*Distributor to the book trade in the United States and Canada*

Rizzoli International Publications Inc.
through St. Martin's Press
175 Fifth Avenue
New York, NY 10010

*Distributor to the art trade in the United States and Canada*

PBC International, Inc.
One School Street
Glen Cove, NY 11542

*Distributor throughout the rest of the world*

Hearst Books International
1350 Avenue of the Americas
New York, NY 10019

Credits appear on pages 186-188 which constitute
an extension of the copyright page.

Library of Congress Cataloging-in-Publication Data

Children's book illustration and design volume 2 / edited by Julie Cummins.
        p.    cm.
    Incluces indexes.
    ISBN 0-86636-393-9
    1.  Illustrated books, Children's.  2. Illustration of books—20th century.
    3.  Illustrators—Biography.  4. Book Design.
I. Cummins, Julie.
NC965.C43   1998
741.6'42 09048—dc20                              91-31457
                                                        CIP

CAVEAT—Information in this text is believed accurate, and will pose
no problem for the student or casual reader. However, the author was
often constrained by information contained in signed release forms,
information that could have been in error or not included at all. Any
misinformation (or lack of information) is the result of failure in these
attestations. The author has done whatever is possible to insure accuracy.

Printed in Hong Kong

10 9 8 7 6 5 4 3 2 1

To the cadre of illustrators
whose artistry and creativity
imbue children's books with
vitality, vibrancy, and pleasure;

To Blair, a perfect illustration
of friendship and support.

# CONTENTS

# INTRODUCTION

"By design"—a phrase that means to fashion according to plan, or to create an image, or to imaginatively craft the look of a finished piece. It is by design that the children's book illustrators selected for inclusion in this book have skillfully arranged and shaped the details which make up a unique work of art—a children's picture book.

The world of children's book illustration, particularly picture books, continues to grow and evolve, adapting new forms and expanding levels of creativity. This specialized artistic field is inviting, rewarding, and some might say, on the "cutting edge". Children's book illustrators are designing wonderfully exciting and appealing art in children's books.

No stylistic approach to picture book illustration is off-limits. Realistic illustration is not the only acceptable style. As illustration and design modes change, picture books reflect these visual innovations and pique childrens' and adults' acuity and curiosity. The variety of illustration styles ranges from the humorous, cartoonish use of line by David Catrow, and the ethnic look reflected in Yumi Heo's work, to the retro look of Dan Yaccarino's poster-like art.

In addition to the range of style, the media utilized by today's illustrators cover the gamut from the pulp paper painting by Denise Fleming to Michael McCurdy's scratchboard art, to the intensely-colored paintings by David Shannon. The fact that many publishers are now identifying the art medium used in the book testifies to the importance attached to illustration.

The illustrators who are included in this volume represent the new wave of artists whose picture book art is visually captivating, intriguing, and noteworthy. The first volume of *Children's Book Illustration and Design* laid the foundation for identifying and recognizing outstanding children's book illustrators by providing a visual showcase of specific illustrations of their work. This accompanying volume builds on that foundation by adding fifty-six more children's book illustrators who are contributing to this provocative field. Each was chosen for their unique style, level of creativity, and recognition by professionals in the children's book arena. Many of the illustrators are award winners, have received critical acclaim, and have had a hand in "animating" this special publishing category.

A 1900 quote from James Gibbons Huneker, an American music critic and writer, in his book, *The Man and His Music*, puts this perspective on the subject: "Scratch an artist and you surprise a child". The artists selected for

Volume II can attest to this; they have all certainly been "scratched" as the books they have created delight and surprise a multitude of children.

Excellence in the field of children's book illustration is recognized through numerous awards in addition to popular acclaim by the intended audience. The most coveted awards are the Caldecott Medal and the Caldecott Honor. The 1997 winner of the Caldecott Medal is David Wisniewski, and his cut-paper illustrations are exemplary of excellence of technique and dramatic effect.

The visual impact and appeal of a book are composed of various design elements including the cover, endpapers, title page, and type treatment. The interaction of elements results in an effect that is greater than any one single part. A picture book that is unified in all the design elements is more appealing and gives a "wholeness" to the book when both text and art work seamlessly together—an aesthetic interplay which is richly demonstrated on the following pages.

Along with the illustration reproductions in both volumes of *Children's Book Illustration and Design* are fascinating comments from the individual artists on what they tried to achieve or why they depicted the story the way they did. In Volume I, Ann Grifalconi, Caldecott Honor recipient for *The Village of Round and Square Houses*, sums up her purpose in the book: "to show that variations in human life do exist, do work, and that there are infinite creative solutions in the world. I hope the book evokes feelings of mystery, wonder, pleasure, and identification."

All of these sentiments recur in the illustrations on the pages ahead. Enjoy them.

—Julie Cummins
*Coordinator, Children's Services*
*The New York Public Library*

# TEDD ARNOLD

Born in Elmira, New York, Tedd Arnold moved with his family to Gainesville, Florida at age ten. His first art lessons in an abandoned dentist's office over The Happy Hour Pool Hall eventually led to a Fine Arts degree from the University of Florida. He and his wife, Carol, started their family in Tallahassee where Mr. Arnold worked as a commercial illustrator. Carol, a kindergarten teacher, drew his attention to children's books. Their first son, Walter, inspired him to write his breakthrough picture book, *No Jumping on the Bed*. Mr. Arnold and his family live, once again, in Elmira.

*Book Title*
*Tracks*

*Author*
**David Galef**

*Publisher*
**Morrow Junior Books**

*Publication Date*
**1996**

*Illustration Medium*
**Watercolor and color pencil**

## TRACKS

When Albert breaks his glasses while supervising the laying of rail-road tracks between two towns, he becomes responsible for one of the most exciting rides that the townspeople have ever had.

. . . . . . . . . . . . . . .

"When I first read *Tracks*, I knew it would be fun to illustrate. It felt like an open, sprawling playground in which I could turn my drawings loose. To me, in a larger sense, the story mirrors the creative process—how an idea sometimes seems to have a mind of its own and as you develop it, you are taken down unexpected pathways until the finished idea is very different from what you had in mind at the start. I love that! Even the creator is surprised by his creation."

# SHONTO W. BEGAY

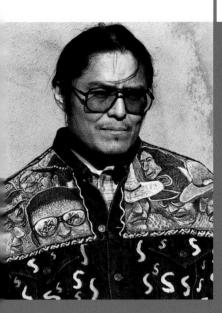

Shonto Begay was born near Shonto, Arizona, the fifth of sixteen children whose father was a Navajo medicine man. He studied fine arts in New Mexico and California, and his work has appeared in more than thirty exhibitions, with many of his paintings now part of permanent museum collections. A committed speaker on Navajo culture, Begay has been interviewed on radio, television, and in a film documentary. He currently lives in Kayenta, Arizona with his wife Cruz and their four children.

## THE MAGIC OF SPIDER WOMAN

Wandering Girl's passion is to weave all the patterns in nature. This is the retelling of the Navajo legend of Spider Woman, a sacred being who taught the Navajo how to weave blankets so they could survive in winter.

• • • • • • • • • • • • • • •

"Spider Woman stories give those of us who benefit from rug weaving an explanation and an opportunity to credit the insect being who made this all ours. They teach us to keep balance in our lives and remind us that people are not gods and are not perfect. . . . I hope this story will encourage readers to search further for Navajo stories and broaden their knowledge about American Indians and their stories. Many people associate Indians with history and guilt. There's more to our culture than that. There are happy things: fantastic legends, storytelling, dancing, music, beautiful arts and crafts."

*Book Title*
**The Magic of Spider Woman**

*Author*
**Shonto W. Begay and
Lois Duncan**

*Publisher*
**Scholastic Inc.**

*Publication Date*
**1996**

*Illustration Medium*
**Watercolor and colored
pencil, ink and graphite,
acrylic paint on canvas**

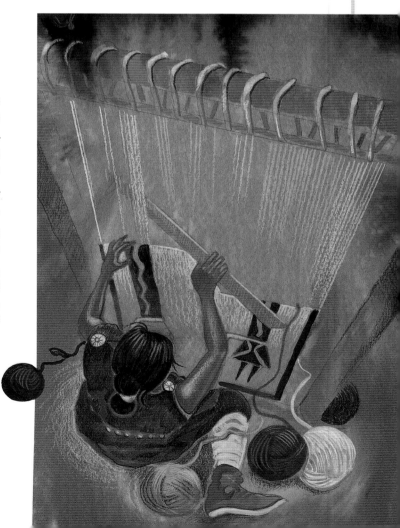

*Book Title*
*Navajo: Visions and Voices Across the Mesa*

*Author*
**Shonto W. Begay**

*Publisher*
**Scholastic Inc.**

*Publication Date*
**1995**

*Illustration Medium*
**Watercolor and colored pencil, ink and graphite, acrylic paint on canvas**

## NAVAJO: VISIONS AND VOICES ACROSS THE MESA

A collection of poems and writings—creation stories, childhood memories, contemporary life, reflections on tribal rituals—about Navajo life on the reservation.

• • • • • • • • • • • • • •

"To re-create facets of my universe in its varying images is the adventure of living. From a very young age, I drew from nature and developed a strong bond with the images around me. . . . Kids ask me where I grew up and how I became an artist. For me, it was finding a place where I could appreciate where I came from. I show them a picture of my story rock. On that particular rock I could taste, smell, and feel the beauty of my surroundings. This gave birth to my first creative energy on this journey. I hope this book will encourage kids to find their own rock or their own story tree, where they can think and draw pictures and read."

# MARÍA CRISTINA BRUSCA

*Book Title*
**On the Pampas**

*Author*
**María Cristina Brusca**

*Publisher*
**Henry Holt and Company, Inc.**

*Publication Date*
**1991**

*Illustration Medium*
**Watercolor**

María Cristina Brusca was born in Buenos Aires, Argentina in 1950. As a child, she lived for long periods of time at her grandparents' ranch on the Argentine pampas and later, in a small ranch purchased and managed by her mother. Since she loved drawing and reading books, Ms. Brusca entered a special high school where she studied drawing, painting, graphic design, and book binding. Ms. Brusca graduated from college in 1973 and became a professor of graphic design. Between 1973 and 1988, she worked in Buenos Aires designing book covers and illustrating children's books. In 1988, she moved to the United States (Kingston, New York), where she established herself as an illustrator and writer of children's books.

# ON THE PAMPAS

• • •

# MY MAMA'S LITTLE RANCH ON THE PAMPAS

This story depicts the authors wonderful first year she spent on the small ranch purchased and managed by her mother. A continuation of *On the Pampas*, about the author's earliest years at her grandparents' ranch.

• • • • • • • • • • • • • •

❝Since I love that big, flat extension of the pampas, the creatures that lived there, the 'gauchos,' their horses, clothes, and way of living, I wanted to share my childhood experiences with American children. In both books, *On the Pampas* and *My Mama's Little Ranch on the Pampas*, I tried to visually describe the landscape, the 'gaucho' culture, and the special rhythm of life in an Argentine ranch from the perspective of a little girl.❞

*Book Title*
**My Mama's Little Ranch on the Pampas**

*Author*
**María Cristina Brusca**

*Publisher*
**Henry Holt and Company, Inc.**

*Publication Date*
**1994**

*Illustration Medium*
**Watercolor**

# MARÍA CRISTINA BRUSCA

*Book Title*
**Three Friends-Tres Amigos**

*Author*
**María Cristina Brusca and
Tona Wilson**

*Publisher*
**Henry Holt and Company, Inc.**

*Publication Date*
**1995**

*Illustration Medium*
**Watercolor**

*Book Title*
**When Jaguars Ate the Moon**

*Author*
**Retold by María Cristina Brusca
and Tona Wilson**

*Publisher*
**Henry Holt and Company, Inc.**

*Publication Date*
**1995**

*Illustration Medium*
**Watercolor**

## THREE FRIENDS-
## TRES AMIGOS

*Three Friends-Tres Amigos* is a bilingual counting book in Spanish and English.

• • • • • • • • • • • • • •

❝In this book I developed a short, funny, visual story to bring the children close to a foreign language. I chose to set up the story in the American Southwest so the children can count characters (animals, plants) familiar to both cultures, such as the coyote or the armadillo. I kept the drawings as simple as I could to help count the characters and follow the action.❞

## WHEN JAGUARS ATE
## THE MOON

*When Jaguars Ate the Moon* is a collection of stories about plants and animals indigenous to the Americas. They are retold and selected from the folklore of twenty-five American cultures.

• • • • • • • • • • • • • •

❝Each page shows a letter, and three animals or plants on the top for children to memorize. There is also a story which came from one specific indigenous group, so I tried to illustrate it through a contemporary drawing comprehensible to the eyes of today's children and, at the same time, truthful to the origin of the tale. Each illustration introduces the landscape, objects used, clothes, houses, and way of life of each culture.❞

# MARK BUEHNER

Mark Buehner has been interested in art from a very early age, and began more serious study as a teenager. Mr. Buehner graduated from Utah State University with a degree in commercial illustration. When the opportunity arrived to create children's picture books, it was a catalyst for Mark to pursue a distinctive style, different from his earlier, more painterly style. The artistic freedom in picture books gives him the opportunity, he says, "to add humor, personality, and even subplots to the written story". *Harvey Potter's Balloon Farm* is an American Library Association Notable Book, an Oppenheim Toy Portfolio Best Book of 1994, and was awarded the National Parenting Publication Gold Medal, 1994. Mark lives in Salt Lake City with his wife Caralyn, and their four children.

*Book Title*
***Harvey Potter's Balloon Farm***

*Author*
**Jerdine Nolen**

*Publisher*
**Lothrop, Lee & Shepard Books**

*Publication Date*
**1994**

*Illustration Medium*
**Oil over acrylic**

## HARVEY POTTER'S BALLOON FARM

A child ventures out in the middle of the night to see how Harvey Potter grows his wonderful balloons.

• • • • • • • • • • • • •

66With my first reading of this book I was immediately attracted by the irresistible combination of a farm and balloons! From a visual standpoint, this story had wonderful possibilities. The challenge was to take the surreal and make it believable and real. I thought in terms of the principles of landscape painting to create depth, and to bring the farm and the balloons to life.99

# DAVID CATROW

David Catrow was born in
Virginia and raised in Ohio.
The second oldest of six
children (four of them sisters),
his most vivid memories are of
his dog Taffy, big pots of
slumgullion and sharing the
family bike—he frequently
tied a broomstick to the frame
to make it a boys' bike. In
college, Mr. Catrow was a
premed major even though
drawing and painting were his
driving force. In addition to
his many illustrated books for
children, he is a nationally
syndicated editorial cartoonist.
Mr. Catrow is the recipient of
*The New York Times* Best
Illustrated Book Award, 1995
for *She's Wearing A Dead Bird
on Her Head*.

*Book Title*
***She's Wearing A Dead Bird on
Her Head***

*Author*
**Kathryn Lasky**

*Publisher*
**Hyperion Books for Children**

*Publication Date*
**1995**

*Illustration Medium*
**Watercolor and ink**

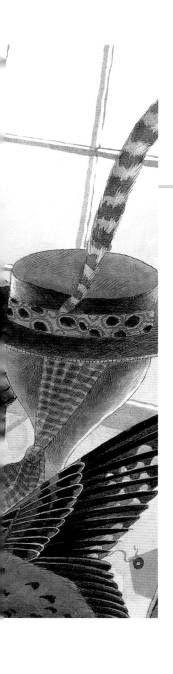

## SHE'S WEARING A DEAD BIRD ON HER HEAD

A fictionalized account of Harriet Hemenway and Minna Hall, founders of the Massachusetts Audubon Society. The two heroic women soar to great heights and distances to save the birds; and for that we tip our hats.

. . . . . . . . . . . . . . . . .

"*She's Wearing A Dead Bird on Her Head* is a special book for me because a bird coincidentally represents my defining moment as an artist. It involved my kindergarten teacher and a realistic rendering of a robin I had done. Her approach to bird art was cold and schematic: a series of circles, triangles and stick legs. The rest of the class drew their birds as instructed, but I couldn't bring myself to do it that way and stood my ground. The teacher prevailed and I spent my snack time with my head down on the table."

# DAVID CATROW

*Book Title*
**The Million-Dollar Bear**

*Author*
**William Kotzwinkle**

*Publisher*
**Alfred A. Knopf, Inc.**

*Publication Date*
**1995**

*Illustration Medium*
**Watercolor**

## THE MILLION-DOLLAR BEAR

After a harrowing escape from the clutches of a miserly millionaire who keeps him in a burglarproof vault, the very valuable original teddy finds a home, and most importantly, his true worth.

● ● ● ● ● ● ● ● ● ● ● ● ●

❝The bear started out as the spitting image of Teddy Roosevelt (where the name 'Teddy Bear' came from), but soon evolved into something more personal. 'TR' was much inclined to take the bull moose by the antlers and get things done. The Million-Dollar Bear, on the other hand, is much more in need of somebody to pick him up out of the dumps, brush him off and give him a little love. 'TR' was very popular in his day, but this bear is a true friend who will never leave your side.❞

# VICTORIA CHESS

*Book Title*
**The Fat Cats At Sea**

*Author*
**J. Patrick Lewis**

*Publisher*
**Apple Soup Books**

*Publication Date*
**1994**

*Illustration Medium*
**Watercolor, techpen, and sepia ink**

"I attended the School of the Museum of Fine Arts, Boston, and due to an overwhelming and pleasurable social life, did not do any work and was asked to leave after two years. Hence, no degree from there or anywhere else. Apart from books, I work now and again for *Cricket*, *Spider*, and *Ladybug* magazines." Today, Ms. Chess lives in Connecticut with her husband, cats, and dogs.

## THE FAT CATS AT SEA

A narrative verse in which the cat crew of The Frisky Dog go to sea in order to bring sticky buns back to the Queen of Catmandoo.

. . . . . . . . . . . . . . .

"The easiest sort of book to do; text and illustrations on facing pages. Since the book has a vertical format, I could not show all of the ship at the same time and keep the cats large enough to be the main focus of the illustrations. Also, several of the poems had many different aspects which I wanted to depict, so I broke these illustrations into smaller ones which still fit in the same frame."

# DAVID CHRISTIANA

"As a child, I saw more professional football players on television than artists so logically, I figured the best way for an adult to make pictures would be to draw and paint during the off-season." Since he fell about a hundred pounds of muscle short of his goal, David Christiana attended Tyler School of Art, Parsons School of Design, and Syracuse University for art instead. Today, Mr. Christiana maintains the philosophy that we are perpetually becoming something. "I still want to make pictures and become an artist," he says, "or a farmer, or a knight, or a lizard, but definitely not a computer."

*Book Title*
**A Tooth Fairy's Tale**

*Author*
**David Christiana**

*Publisher*
**Farrar, Straus & Giroux, Inc.**

*Publication Date*
**1995**

*Illustration Medium*
**Watercolor**

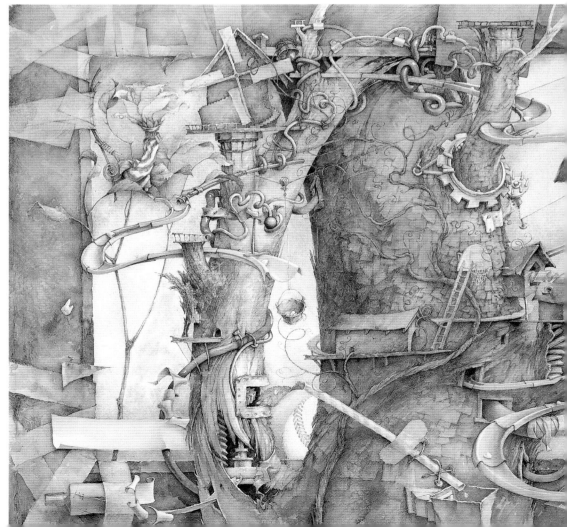

## A TOOTH FAIRY'S TALE

A tooth fairy and her father, the sandman, rescue her mother who has been turned into stone by a giant, who is actually a boy.

• • • • • • • • • • • • • •

66This was originally a story about the sandwitch and the sandman and the Sweet Dreams baby's tooth processing plant. But, once the tooth fairy got involved, she refocused the whole thing (that little stinker). I enjoyed letting a child be the giant in this tale. Since dreams do come in sweet and sour flavors, this seemed true to me.99

## DRAWER IN A DRAWER

Fud Butter draws and tows a line that becomes a box, catches the moon, reaches the top of the sky and ends up back in his dresser drawer.

· · · · · · · · · · · · · · ·

"The character of Fud Butter jumped from my sketchbook on a flight somewhere over the American Southwest. To me, he personifies an imagination unfettered. Fud Butter tows his line through a carousel of pictures and words. I chose oil paint on paper sized with egg yolk to maintain the tactile and visceral qualities of the sketches which poke through now and then. Making the paintings smaller than the book was also an attempt to draw the viewer closer to the drawing and painting process."

# GOOD GRISELLE

Angels and gargoyles test a woman's goodness by providing her with an ugly baby to love.

. . . . . . . . . . . . . .

**"**Jane Yolen wrote a beautiful story so, this was just plain old fun to illustrate. I simply painted what I saw as well as I was able. Besides, how could I resist an ugly child, angels, and gargoyles?**"**

*Book Title*
**Good Griselle**

*Author*
**Jane Yolen**

*Publisher*
**Harcourt Brace & Company**

*Publication Date*
**1994**

*Illustration Medium*
**Watercolor**

*Book Title*
**Drawer In A Drawer**

*Author*
**David Christiana**

*Publisher*
**Farrar, Straus & Giroux, Inc.**

*Publication Date*
**1990**

*Illustration Medium*
**Oil on paper with egg yolk**

# ALEXANDRA DAY

*Book Title*
*Carl's Christmas*

*Author*
**Alexandra Day**

*Publisher*
**Farrar, Straus & Giroux, Inc.**

*Publication Date*
**1990**

*Illustration Medium*
**Oil paint**

"My mother gardened and canned and decorated and ordered with knowledge, precision, and grace. She taught me these things, which helped me to grow up with the realization that I could make the home and the world more orderly and beautiful." Alexandra Day was born in Cincinnati, Ohio. Ms. Day lived from the ages of nine to thirteen on a farm in Kentucky. She was immersed in an atmosphere of "idealistic perfectionism" as a student at Swarthmore College, and took two art courses at New York's Art Students League. In 1967, she married Harold Darling with whom she produced the publishing company, The Green Tiger Press. In 1986, it gestated into The Blue Lantern Studio, a firm that created visual books for many publishers and enabled Ms. Day to experience the process of producing books firsthand.

# CARL'S CHRISTMAS

Carl and the baby have Christmas adventures, including meeting Santa Claus, while mother and father have gone to church with Grandma.

• • • • • • • • • • • • • •

❝I wanted to convey the magic and depth that Christmas brings, as well as the messages of goodwill and charity. I always preferred to render Carl himself with oil, but the night venue of this book made oil seem appropriate for the entire story, and successfully conveyed the feelings I desired.❞

# ALEXANDRA DAY

*Book Title*
**Carl's Afternoon in the Park**

*Author*
**Alexandra Day**

*Publisher*
**Farrar, Straus & Giroux, Inc.**

*Publication Date*
**1991**

*Illustration Medium*
**Watercolor**

## CARL'S AFTERNOON IN THE PARK

Mother leaves Carl in charge of the baby and puppy and they have a fine romp until mother returns to find them unmoved.

• • • • • • • • • • • • • •

"Because this book takes place entirely outdoors, I attempted to make each illustration work both as a successful landscape painting and be able to carry the narrative message which, in a wordless book, is a necessary part of each illustration."

# FRANK AND ERNEST PLAY BALL

An elephant and a bear manage a minor-league baseball team for a day and learn about cooperation, responsibility, and baseball slang in the process.

● ● ● ● ● ● ● ● ● ● ● ● ● ● ● ●

"I used a combination of watercolor for the backgrounds and secondary figures, and oil for the main characters, Frank and Ernest. Using oils accomplishes two things—it helps make figures more solid and imposing as befits two large animals, and allows me more control in achieving skin and fur."

*Book Title*
*Frank and Ernest Play Ball*

*Author*
**Alexandra Day**

*Publisher*
**Scholastic Inc.**

*Publication Date*
**1990**

*Illustration Medium*
**Watercolor and oil**

After graduating from Parsons School of Design, Leo and Diane Dillon began their collaboration—an alliance which they refer to as "the third artist," who creates something different than either of them would do separately. They taught materials and techniques at the School of Visual Arts for seven years in the early 1970s. "Techniques are to us what words are to a writer; they are a means to express our thoughts". Leo and Diane Dillon are recipients of the Caldecott Medal in consecutive years, 1976 and 1977, and are the United States nominees for the International Hans Christian Award, 1996, for the body of their work.

## PISH, POSH, SAID HIERONYMUS BOSCH

An imaginative poem about the fifteenth-century painter, Hieronymus Bosch, filled with beasts and creatures.

• • • • • • • • • • • • • •

❝The inspiration for this book was the art of Hieronymous Bosch. We painted in acrylic on acetate and glazed with oils. Our son, Lee, joined the collaboration, creating the frame using bronze, brass, wood, silver, and copper. He also painted on the illustrations. Illustrating this book was enjoyable because we had the freedom to invent a variety of zany creatures.❞

Book Title
*Pish, Posh, Said Hieronymus Bosch*

Author
**Nancy Willard**

Publisher
**Harcourt Brace & Company**

Publication Date
**1991**

Illustration Medium
**Acrylic and oil on acetate/frame of bronze, copper, silver, brass and wood**

*Book Title*
**The Sorcerer's Apprentice**

*Author*
**Nancy Willard**

*Publisher*
**The Blue Sky Press**

*Publication Date*
**1993**

*Illustration Medium*
**Watercolor on Arches hot press**

## THE SORCERER'S APPRENTICE

Sylvia, the new apprentice to the great magician, Tottibo, steals one of his spells to complete an impossible task and accidentally creates chaos.

· · · · · · · · · · · · · · ·

66 This tale has been told in many forms: as an ancient story, a poem, and as a film. For Nancy's retelling, there were no limits on any particular time setting nor any technical requirements, so we gave our imagination free reign. There were no special research problems since we were already familiar with the tools and materials a dressmaker uses. The watercolor technique gave us a light and airy feeling we felt was appropriate for this fairy tale. 99

"When I was nineteen and working in the orange groves on a kibbutz, I realized what I wanted to do in my life—write, draw, and paint. ...One of my first books, *Chicken Man*, takes place on a kibbutz and won the National Jewish Book Award. A full circle." Michelle Edwards was born in Bridgeport, Connecticut, and grew up in upstate New York. She earned her Bachelor of Arts at the State University of New York at Albany, and studied at the Bazalel Art Academy in Jerusalem and received a Master of Arts as well as a Master of Fine Arts from the University of Iowa in printmaking. She now resides in St. Paul, Minnesota with her husband and three daughters.

*Book Title*
**Eve and Smithy**

*Author*
**Michelle Edwards**

*Publisher*
**Lothrop, Lee & Shepard Books**

*Publication Date*
**1994**

*Illustration Medium*
**Gouache and watercolor**

## EVE AND SMITHY

Smithy tries to think of a gift for Eve, his neighbor and friend who gardens and paints.

● ● ● ● ● ● ● ● ● ● ● ● ● ●

"Since Eve and Smithy are the only characters in this story and since most of the action takes place outside, between, and in their gardens, I had to battle those limitations in order to give the book some variety and life. Changing the point of view, going close in and moving back as well as concentrating on different colors in each spread helped me create a sense of differentiation between the illustrations."

# MICHELLE EDWARDS

Book Title
*A Baker's Portrait*

Author
**Michelle Edwards**

Publisher
**Lothrop, Lee & Shepard Books**

Publication Date
**1991**

Illustration Medium
**Gouache and watercolor**

Book Title
*Chicken Man*

Author
**Michelle Edwards**

Publisher
**Lothrop, Lee & Shepard Books**

Publication Date
**1991**

Illustration Medium
**Gouache and watercolor**

## A BAKER'S PORTRAIT

Michelin paints portraits that do not flatter her sitters, but learns an enduring lesson when she must paint her kindly aunt and uncle.

. . . . . . . . . . . . . . . . .

❝Michelin the portrait painter who always paints exactly what she sees, warts and all, must paint her beloved, but fat and ugly, aunt and uncle. How should she paint them? Her problem became mine, too. How to paint corpulent, unsightly, but kind people? It was a struggle. I studied many faces to figure out what makes a face ugly or warm-hearted. Often, it was the eyes, kind eyes that mirror the soul and shine forth even in the ugliest of faces.❞

## CHICKEN MAN

Each time Chicken Man moves into a new job on the kibbutz, someone else wants to take over his job. As a consequence, the chickens suffer.

. . . . . . . . . . . . . . . . .

❝Like Chicken Man, I too, worked in a kibbutz chicken coop. However, I hated the chickens. How could I portray them as Chicken Man saw them—lovable? I finally began to think of the chickens as young children, maybe my own children, always wanting to be near, always fluttering about, always full of life. . . lovable each in their own way.❞

# LISA CAMPBELL ERNST

"Growing up in Oklahoma, I had the good fortune to be a part of a family that believed books were not only important, but fun. Especially lucky for me, my parents believed in the importance of reading aloud, and from this I grew to love books." When Lisa Campbell Ernst began illustrating books, she quickly discovered she also wanted to "draw with words," and so became an author as well as an illustrator. Ms. Ernst received her Bachelor of Fine Arts from the Univesity of Oklahoma.

## GINGER JUMPS

Ginger, a young circus dog, searches for a little girl to love and a family to live with.

· · · · · · · · · · · · · · ·

66 The challenge of illustrating *Ginger Jumps* was in creating the hustle-bustle of the circus world in a silent, two-dimensional medium. Ginger is a small dog who is both figuratively and literally enveloped by the circus. Using busy compositions filled with details, colors, and textures, I tried to communicate Ginger's circus environment. Near the end of the book, when the pace suddenly changes and the spotlight shines on Ginger, who pauses at the top of a huge staircase, the illustrations change as well, becoming stark and 'quiet,' in an attempt to communicate that heart-pounding stillness to the reader. 99

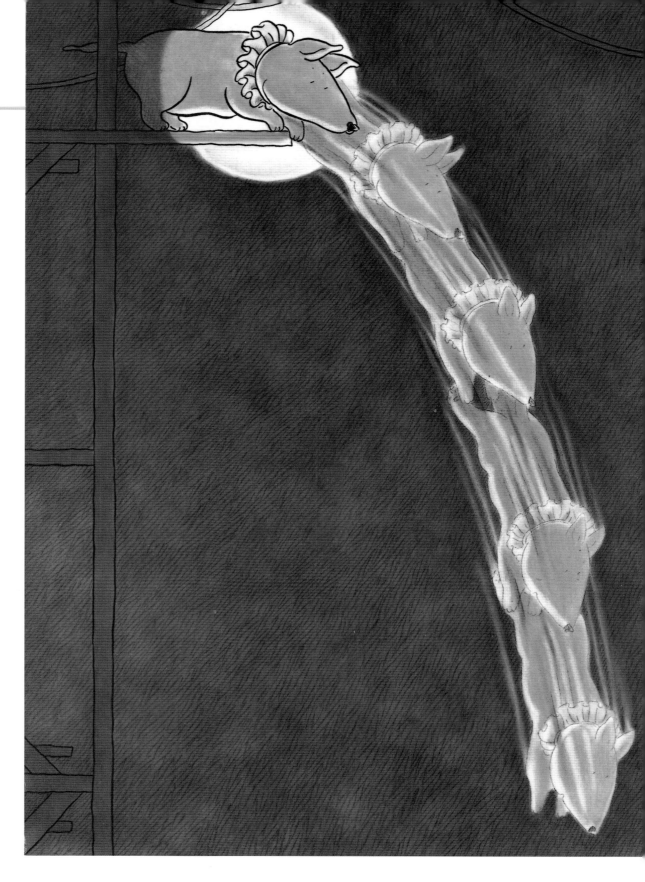

*Book Title*
**Ginger Jumps**

*Author*
**Lisa Campbell Ernst**

*Publisher*
**Simon & Schuster Books
for Young Readers**

*Publication Date*
**1990**

*Illustration Medium*
**Pastel, ink, and pencil**

# LISA CAMPBELL ERNST

Book Title
*When Bluebell Sang*

Author
**Lisa Campbell Ernst**

Publisher
**Simon & Schuster Books
for Young Readers**

Publication Date
**1989**

Illustration Medium
**Pastel, ink and pencil**

Book Title
*Little Red Riding Hood:*
*A Newfangled Prairie Tale*

Author
**Lisa Campbell Ernst**

Publisher
**Simon & Schuster Books
for Young Readers**

Publication Date
**1995**

Illustration Medium
**Pastel, ink and pencil**

# WHEN BLUEBELL SANG

Bluebell, a singing cow, and Swenson, her farmer, are taken on the road by the greedy talent agent, Big Eddie. Fame quickly follows, but Bluebell and Swenson long for their home on the farm, and finally trick Big Eddie in order to return there.

• • • • • • • • • • • • • •

❝The fun of illustrating *When Bluebell Sang* was in visually creating a time long past. After choosing the year 1916, I visited libraries, museums, and flea markets, gathering research on everything from train stations to wallpaper, pincushions to postcards. Of course, Bluebell did not actually exist. But one of the many jobs of an illustrator is to help the reader make that transition from the 'real' world to the fantasy world. I believe that the information gleaned from the right research helps build the bridge to enable the reader to do just that.❞

# LITTLE RED RIDING HOOD: A NEWFANGLED PRAIRIE TALE

This is an updated version of *Little Red Riding Hood* set on the Midwestern prairie. Red Riding Hood and her grandmother are feisty heroines who naturally outwit a not-so-clever wolf.

• • • • • • • • • • • • • •

❝The Little Red Riding Hood of this *Newfangled Prairie Tale* version is not your normal Little Red Riding Hood. The illustrations are what first clues us into this—we see Little Red Riding Hood, in a red sweatshirt with hood, riding her bike along a prairie road. I felt the characters needed to look a bit off-the-wall, a bit goofy. I also tried to communicate the openness and light that one feels on the prairie—mirroring Little Red Riding Hood's carefree feelings, and contrast that visually with the wolf, who is dark and menacing, and disrupts the landscape, as well as the tranquility of the day.❞

# DENISE FLEMING

Denise Fleming graduated with an illustration major from Kendall College of Art and Design in 1971. Since then, she embarked on a freelance career and began illustrating for advertising, the toy and craft fields, and mass market books. Ms. Fleming's pulp-painting style debuted in 1991 in her first book as an author illustrator, *In the Tall, Tall Grass*. She has twice received Notable Children's Book citations for *Lunch* and *In the Small, Small Pond*, which was also awarded a Caldecott Honor Award in 1994.

*Book Title*
**In the Small, Small Pond**

*Author*
**Denise Fleming**

*Publisher*
**Henry Holt and Company, Inc.**

*Publication Date*
**1993**

*Illustration Medium*
**Pulp painting using cotton rag fiber**

# IN THE SMALL, SMALL POND

This story describes the activities of the wild creatures that live in and around a pond as seasons pass.

• • • • • • • • • • • • • •

"I wanted to present an up close view of pond life in order for the reader to be completely surrounded by the images. For this reason, I chose double-page spreads with full bleeds and integrated the text into the illustrations, using earth tones alongside vibrant primary colors. Strong color outlines helped pop the images, and pulp painting allowed me to create mottled areas of color in the water and textures, such as fur and the sand of the pond bank."

Book Title
*Lunch*

*Author*
**Denise Fleming**

*Publisher*
**Henry Holt and Company, Inc.**

*Publication Date*
**1992**

*Illustration Medium*
**Pulp painting using cotton rag fiber**

## LUNCH

A small, very hungry mouse helps himself to a large array of colorful fruits and vegetables.

. . . . . . . . . . . . . . .

66 *Lunch* is a book about color, so using strong, vibrant colors was my first consideration. To accentuate the colors, a black-and-white tablecloth was used as a constant. This tablecloth became the stage for the mouse's antics. To create movement, I changed the angle of the table from page to page. The colors chosen for the backgrounds move through the color spectrum. The book begins on white—all color, and ends on black—absence of color. 99

## BARNYARD BANTER

*Barnyard Banter* introduces the lively, noisy animals of the barnyard. All the animals are where they should be except the goose, who's off chasing a bright yellow butterfly.

• • • • • • • • • • • • • • • •

66To create the gritty texture of the barnyard and surrounding fields, I added various materials to the paper pulp before pouring the images. Crushed tea leaves were added to the pulp to create the sand/dirt texture of the rooster's yard. Alfalfa hay was added to the pasture pulp, coffee grounds were added to the wallow pulp, and straw was added to the hayloft pulp. To simulate the wire fence of the peacock pen, I used a string sack that formerly held tomatoes.99

*Book Title*
**Barnyard Banter**

*Author*
**Denise Fleming**

*Publisher*
**Henry Holt and Company, Inc.**

*Publication Date*
**1992**

*Illustration Medium*
**Pulp painting using cotton rag fiber**

# FIONA FRENCH

Fiona French was born in the west of England, in 1944, and educated in Devon. Ms. French trained to be a painter at Croydon College of Art, in South London, and began writing and illustrating books in 1968. She published her first book in 1970. Twenty-six of her picture books have been published since then, and in 1986 she became the recipient of the Kate Greenaway Award. An exhibition of Fiona French's illustrations and paintings takes place every other year at a gallery in Norfolk.

*Book Title*
**King of Another Country**

*Author*
**Fiona French**

*Publisher*
**Scholastic Inc.**

*Publication Date*
**1992**

*Illustration Medium*
**Gouache and crayon**

## ANANCY AND MR. DRY-BONE

Based on characters from Jamaican and African folktales, rich Mr. Dry-Bone and penniless Anancy both set out to marry Miss Louise. All his animal friends help Anancy win the day.

• • • • • • • • • • • • • •

"Bright colors, used with black, white and grays, allowed me to portray the atmosphere of the West Indies."

*Book Title*
**Anancy and Mr. Dry-Bone**

*Author*
**Fiona French**

*Publisher*
**Little, Brown and Company**

*Publication Date*
**1991**

*Illustration Medium*
**Gouache, watercolor, and crayon**

## KING OF ANOTHER COUNTRY

In an African village, a man named Ojo never helps anyone. When the King of the Forest offers to make Ojo the king of another land, he learns to be a gracious and good king.

• • • • • • • • • • • • • •

"African textiles inspired me—the colors were used to give an impression of rich vegetation and create the sense of a hot, dry exotic country."

Born in Los Angeles in 1935, Mr. Gerstein attended the Chouinard Institute of Art there before moving to New York City where he lived and worked for twenty-five years making animated films for television. His independently produced short film, *The Magic Magic Ring*, won a Cine Golden Eagle in 1968, and his animated video film, *Beauty and the Beast*, won a Cine Golden Eagle and the American Film Foundation Award for Best Children's Video, 1989. In 1971, Mr. Gerstein collaborated with author Elizabeth Levy to create the *Something Queer is Going On* series of mystery books for Delacorte Publishing. He began writing and illustrating his own books in 1980, and in 1987, *The Mountains of Tibet* was awarded *The New York Times* Best Illustrated Book Award.

*Book Title*
**The Story of May**

*Author*
**Mordicai Gerstein**

*Publisher*
**HarperCollins Publishers**

*Publication Date*
**1993**

*Illustration Medium*
**Watercolor on Arches paper**

## THE STORY OF MAY

The month of May, portrayed as a little girl, visits her relatives—all the other months.

• • • • • • • • • • • • • •

66 Portraying each month as a person was fun. Transparent watercolor was chosen for its lightness and luminosity. This medium has inherent limitations, however, which include its unforgivingness, which must be overcome and turned to advantage. 99

# MORDICAI GERSTEIN

## THE MOUNTAINS OF TIBET
A woodcutter grows up and dies in Tibet, and chooses a new life via reincarnation.

• • • • • • • • • • • • • • • •

"I studied Tibetan painting before choosing gouache for this book. I didn't want to imitate Tibetan art, but to refer to it. All the pictures were very difficult, even the small ones at the beginning of the story. The Mandala-like pictures took a lot of time and care, and even the blue-gray background color required much trial and error."

Book Title
**The Mountains of Tibet**

Author
**Mordicai Gerstein**

Publisher
**HarperCollins Publishers**

Publication Date
**1987**

Illustration Medium
**Gouache on Arches paper**

# CARLA GOLEMBE

Carla Golembe has been a painter and printmaker for over twenty years, and an illustrator since 1990. At Kalani Home Cultural Center in Hawaii, Ms. Golembe was an artist in residence. Currently, she exhibits her artwork nationally and internationally, and her pieces are included in a number of collections including Hyatt Corporation, Pan Pacific Hotels, and Medical College of Virginia Hospitals. Her work has also appeared in magazines and on CD covers. Ms. Golembe won *The New York Times* Best Illustrated Award in 1992 for *Why The Sky is Far Away*. She enjoys dance, music, snorkeling and tropical travel.

## WHY THE SKY IS FAR AWAY

The sky was once so close to the earth that people cut parts of it to eat, but their waste and greed caused the sky to move far away.

• • • • • • • • • • • • • •

**66** *Why The Sky is Far Away* was my first book, so part of the challenge and excitement was working with flow and continuity. I had, as a visual artist, been using imagery from Nigerian drumming and dance, which I studied while working on the story to immerse myself in the feeling of the culture. Working with monotype, one of my two main mediums, seemed appropriate for creating the large, bold areas of translucent color. The message of the story—respect for nature and the environment—was very important to me. I hoped to inspire in the reader a sense of vibrant colors, magic, and visual rhythm. I wanted, in this and in all my books, to combine key elements of the culture with my imagination to produce unique images. **99**

*Book Title*
**Why the Sky is Far Away**

*Author*
**Mary-Joan Gerson**

*Publisher*
**Little, Brown and Company**

*Publication Date*
**1992**

*Illustration Medium*
**Monotype**

Julia Gorton is an illustrator, designer, and teacher at Parson's School of Design, and the mother of three small children. She has worked as an art director at Rodale, Fairchild, and Condé Nast. Her illustrations have been featured in shows at the Society of Illustrators, and the Society of Publication Designers. After living for fifteen years in Manhattan, Ms. Gorton moved recently to the quieter suburbs of New Jersey. She still likes to travel with her husband and children, go on antique collecting exhibitions, and dig in the family garden.

## RIDDLE RHYMES

A collection of fifteen "who am I" and "what am I" rhyming riddles.

. . . . . . . . . . . . . . . . .

**"**The text of *Riddle Rhymes* presented me with the problem of illustrating riddles, which, if the pictures were too literal and obvious, would spoil the surprise for the reader. I therefore had to visualize more metaphoric or symbolic solutions to the illustration problem, while keeping the pictures bright, clean, and fun. In order to vary as much as possible issues of color, scale, and detail in the illustrations, I kept the design of the book simple allowing it to showcase the individual paintings and the unique challenges of solving each riddle.**"**

## THE GUMDROP TREE

When her father gives her a bag of colorful, sugary gumdrops to eat, a little girl decides to plant them instead.

• • • • • • • • • • • • • •

66In this, my first picture book, I attempted to use a strong design sense to make the illustrations and type more striking and harmonious. Most picture books are designed in an assembly-line fashion by overworked company emloyees who have little affinity for the work of the illustrator. But in *The Gumdrop Tree*, I was able to design the type, layout, cover, and illustrations myself to create a book with an overall visual integrity, and a look that makes it distinctive in the marketplace. The book is, therefore, kid friendly and visually sophisticated at the same time.99

*Book Title*
***The Gumdrop Tree***

*Author*
**Elizabeth Spurr**

*Publisher*
**Hyperion Books for Children**

*Publication Date*
**1994**

*Illustration Medium*
**Airbrushed acrylic on paper**

*Book Title*
**Riddle Rhymes**

*Author*
**Charles Ghigna**

*Publisher*
**Hyperion Books for Children**

*Publication Date*
**1996**

*Illustration Medium*
**Airbrushed acrylic on paper**

# MARY GRANDPRÉ

Mary GrandPré has freelanced for fifteen years. She works out of her home on a variety of projects ranging from children's books to corporate brochures, and her work can be seen in *Communications Arts*, *Graphis*, *Society of Illustrators*, and *Print* magazines. Ms. GrandPré attended the Minneapolis College of Art and Design. She judged a Society of Illustration show, a Society of Los Angeles Illustrators' Competition, and served as a visiting speaker at the Buffalo Art Directors' Club, and Ringling School.

*Book Title*
**The Thread of Life**

*Author*
**Dominic Vitorini**

*Publisher*
**Crown Publishers, Inc.**

*Publication Date*
**1995**

*Illustration Medium*
**Pastel on paper**

## THE THREAD OF LIFE

A collection of twelve Italian tales, written and retold in fable form, each with a comical twist and a moral message.

· · · · · · · · · · · · · ·

66I approached *The Thread of Life* as a collection of separate stories, each with its own characters, but holding them together in style and design. The major challenge was to create a variety of old Italian costumes, settings, and characters in reference to historical specifications without becoming too serious.99

# MARY GRANDPRÉ

*Book Title*
**Chin Yu Min and the Ginger Cat**

*Author*
**Jennifer Armstrong**

*Publisher*
**Crown Publishers, Inc.**

*Publication Date*
**1993**

*Illustration Medium*
**Pastel on paper**

## CHIN YU MIN AND THE GINGER CAT

An old woman has a change of heart and becomes a loving friend to a cat after the cat gets lost and she frantically searches for him.

• • • • • • • • • • • • • • •

"Since *Chin Yu Min and the Ginger Cat* was my first book, I didn't have any set way of approaching it. I took the psychological role of a movie director, moving around the sets and creating a variety of angles and perspectives. I wanted to create a believable setting of ancient China, and most importantly, I wanted to evoke an emotional involvement and empathy for the characters."

"The world is a carousel of images that take on meaning and poetry," Wendy Anderson Halperin explains, "and every artist that has influenced me affects the way I see this carousel of images." Ms. Halperin attended Syracuse University and Pratt Institute. Her work includes illustrations for the advertising agencies Leo Burnett, and Benton & Bowles, in addition to portrait painting and fine art painting. For her children's book illustrations, she is the recipient of the Marion Vanett Ridgway Honor Book Award, *The New York Times* Notable Book of the Year (twice), *Boston Globe* Best Book of the Year Award, New York Public Library's 100 Best Books of the Year Award, and the School Library Journal Best Book of 1993.

## HOMEPLACE

Here is a story almost 200 years long, and all of it happens in one house that from year to year has grown and changed and gathered in one family, from great-great-great-great grandpa to a child today.

. . . . . . . . . . . . . .

**66** I enjoyed describing the interconnection of generations of a family and how each generation inspired the next. My ultimate goal was to portray family members caring about each other. **99**

*Book Title*
**Homeplace**

*Author*
**Anne Shelby**

*Publisher*
**Orchard Books**

*Publication Date*
**1995**

*Illustration Medium*
**Pencil and watercolor**

## WHEN CHICKENS GROW TEETH

A large, lovable Frenchman is married to a vile tempered woman named Madame Colette. He falls, and bedridden, is doomed to hatching chicken eggs under his arms which he grows to love. Adapted from a story by Guy de Maupassant.

• • • • • • • • • • • • • •

❝The essence of this book and images to me is—no matter what the circumstances are, make the best of it.❞

*Book Title*
**When Chickens Grow Teeth**

*Author*
**Wendy Anderson Halperin**

*Publisher*
**Orchard Books**

*Publication Date*
**1996**

*Illustration Medium*
**Pencil and watercolor**

# YUMI HEO

Yumi Heo was born and raised in Korea. Her art experience started when she was four or five when her mother bought her "a box of crayons," she says, encouraging her to draw throughout childhood. In 1989, Ms. Heo came to the United States. She later received a Master of Fine Arts in illustration from the School of Visual Arts. Ms Heo's editorial illustrations have been published in *The New Yorker*, *House Beautiful*, *Child*, *McCall's*, *Condé Nast Traveler*, *Shape*, *Troica*, *Wired* and *Bloomberg* magazines, as well as *The Boston Globe*.

## ONE AFTERNOON

A boy goes out to many different stores with his mother and listens to varying sounds. Each store and place they visit has a sound that is specific to the location.

• • • • • • • • • • • • • • • •

"My illustrations interpret the mood underlying the text. My approach for this book was to capture the moment for Minho at each store. The artwork, particularly the use of different typefaces, is different for every sound; for example, the type treatment for the sounds of fire engine sirens starts small and grows larger, to elicit how you would feel as the sound gets louder."

# THE RABBIT'S ESCAPE

The rabbit is one of the most prevalent characters in Korean folk tales. In this adaptation of a tale that appears in *Korean Folk and Fairy Tales*, a sick underwater dragon king needs to eat a rabbit's liver in order to get well, and the chosen rabbit shrewdly escapes.

• • • • • • • • • • • • •

"After I read the stories, I became a voyager of imagination. My illustrations are not based on a realistic perspective in the Rabbit books. . . I want children to see my illustrations and to know that they can experiment, and that they can draw the animals the same way that I drew them. I want them to feel very close to their imaginations."

*Book Title*
**The Rabbit's Escape**

*Author*
**Suzanne Crowder Han**

*Publisher*
**Henry Holt and Company, Inc.**

*Publication Date*
**1995**

*Illustration Medium*
**Oil, pencil, and collage**

*Book Title*
**One Afternoon**

*Author*
**Yumi Heo**

*Publisher*
**Orchard Books**

*Publication Date*
**1994**

*Illustration Medium*
**Oil, pencil, and collage**

# STEPHEN T. JOHNSON

Stephen T. Johnson was born in Madison, Wisconsin, and grew up in Bordeaux, France, and Lawrence, Kansas. Mr. Johnson credits his father as the person that inspired him to find unique beauty in places where others might not look for it. Mr. Johnson received his Bachelor of Fine Arts in painting from the University of Kansas, and now lives and works as an illustrator and painter in Brooklyn, New York. He has illustrated magazine covers for *Time*, *Forbes*, and *The New Yorker* as well as CD covers. In addition to being featured at the Society of Illustrators Museum and numerous exhibitions across the country, Mr. Johnson is the recipient of the Caldecott Honor Book Award, 1996.

*Book Title*
**Hoops**

*Author*
**Robert Burleigh**

*Publisher*
**Harcourt Brace & Company**

*Publication Date*
**1997**

*Illustration Medium*
**Pastel on Ingres paper**

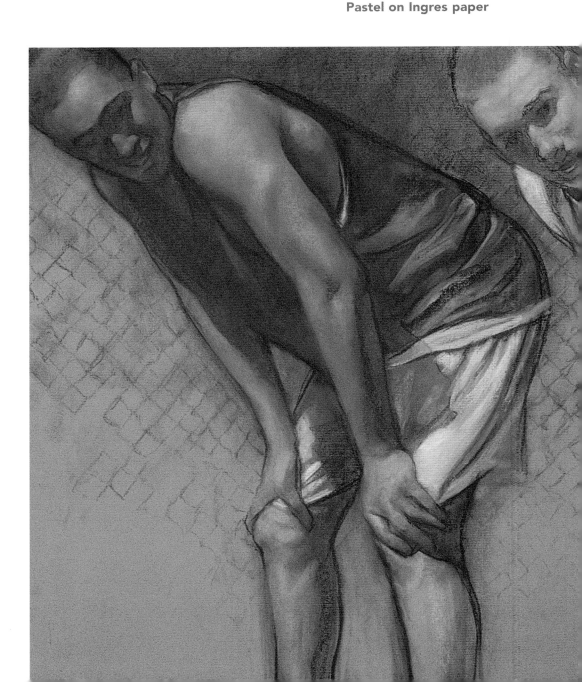

## HOOPS

Poetic text and dynamic pictures capture the energy and passion of the frozen moments that make a basketball game.

• • • • • • • • • • • • • •

❝*Hoops* offered me the chance to push my art in a very exciting direction—also an opportunity to do figures in motion. I think the art captures the poetry of the actions and the energy of the game; there's a simplicity and unfinished quality to the illustrations that says a lot. I used the exercise of drawing with my left hand (although I'm right handed) in preparation for the life drawings. I hoped to convey a contemporary, yet classic feel.❞

# STEPHEN T. JOHNSON

## THE GIRL WHO WANTED A SONG

Maria, a lonely orphan, discovers that she has a song to sing when she encounters and befriends a Canadian goose.

• • • • • • • • • • • • • • •

"I intended to create a magical book—a book with images about dreams, evocative skies and lush, green vegetation; a setting that would be just right for Steve Sanfield's beautiful tale of friendship between a young girl and a goose. I chose a combination of watercolor and pastel on different colored papyrus, which added a sense of luminosity to the images."

Book Title
*The Tie Man's Miracle:*
*A Chanukah Tale*

Author
**Stephen Schnur**

Publisher
**Morrow Junior Books**

Publication Date
**1995**

Illustration Medium
**Watercolor on paper**

Book Title
*The Girl Who Wanted A Song*

Author
**Steve Sanfield**

Publisher
**Harcourt Brace & Company**

Publication Date
**1996**

Illustration Medium
**Watercolor and pastel on colored paper**

## THE TIE MAN'S MIRACLE: A CHANUKAH TALE

On the last night of Chanukah, after hearing of how an old man lost his family in the Holocaust, a young man makes a wish for the return of the "tie man's" family. The wish is carried to God as the menorah candles burn down.

● ● ● ● ● ● ● ● ● ● ● ● ● ●

**❝**I chose to illustrate this story for its strong narrative and sensitive handling of the Holocaust. With regard to the images, I wanted to convey a gentle and emotional quality concentrating on the physical gestures and facial expressions of the characters. I also wanted to have fun with the patterns like the falling snow and the ties. Watercolor seemed perfect; it kept the art simple and delicate.**❞**

Steve Johnson and Lou Fancher, a husband and wife prize-winning team of artists, began illustrating children's books in 1989, when Knopf asked them to illustrate *No Star Nights*. Initially collaborating in the conceptual aspect of their artwork, Mr. Johnson and Ms. Fancher gradually developed a unique approach wherein both artists conceive, draw, design and paint. They began creating children's books under their primary roles as illustrator and designer, with subsequent books reflecting the interactive approach that distinguishes them as a creative team. They live and work in Minneapolis, Minnesota.

*Book Title*
**The Salamander Room**

*Author*
**Anne Mazer**

*Publisher*
**Alfred A. Knopf, Inc.**

*Publication Date*
**1991**

*Illustration Medium*
**Oil on paper**

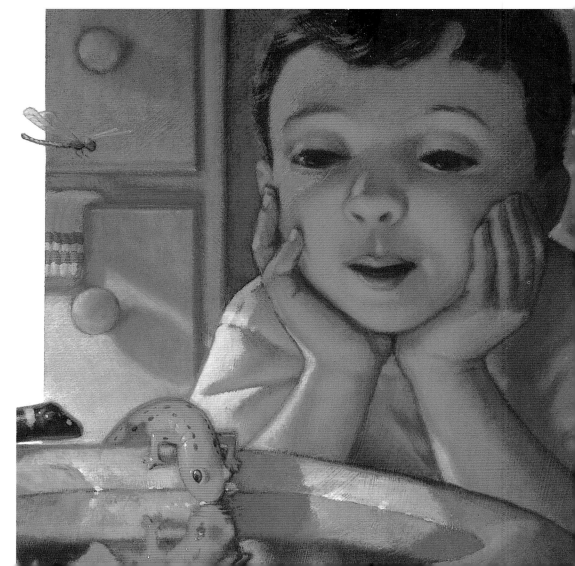

## THE SALAMANDER ROOM

A young boy, Brian, finds a salamander and thinks of the many things he can do to make a perfect home for it.

• • • • • • • • • • • • • • •

" *The Salamander Room* gave us the opportunity to illustrate some of our favorite things: trees, birds, bugs, moonlight, and a young person with a fantastic imagination. We chose rich greens and blues to create a plush environment, and designed compositions progressing from contained images to full-page spreads to parallel the transformation of Brian's room. Making the salamander a loveable character was important to us; we gave it active positions, a bright orange color and slightly larger-than realistic eyes. We explored the woods, often getting down on 'salamander level' to see nature from a different perspective. The cover design was stimulated by Lou's view from our studio—a vine covered chimney on the house next door. "

# STEVE JOHNSON & LOU FANCHER

*Book Title*
*My Many Colored Days*

*Author*
**Dr. Seuss**

*Publisher*
**Alfred A. Knopf, Inc.**

*Publication Date*
**1996**

*Illustration Medium*
**Acrylic on canvas**

## MY MANY COLORED DAYS

This rhyming story describes each day in terms of a particular color which, in turn, is associated with specific emotions.

● ● ● ● ● ● ● ● ● ● ● ● ● ● ●

66Initially, our approach to *My Many Colored Days* was the same as for any book—we read the manuscript over and over. We gathered a vast collection of Dr. Seuss books, discussed painting styles and overall design, then tossed about first-impression images stimulated by the text. Dr. Seuss' fame could have been an enormous obstacle in our path, but his stated desire for a new approach gave us the impetus for exploration. Inuit sculpture, folk art, modern art, and the work of Matisse all influenced the painting style we developed. To complement the text, the forms were kept simple and the color was applied expressively. Because we wanted the type to be active but not busy, we used primarily Helvetica. Letter forms and words were then stretched, pulled and manipulated to reflect the mood of the art and text. The word, 'wheee' became the one exception when we fell in love with the bee-shaped form of Bellevue 'eeee's'.99

# G. BRIAN KARAS

G. Brian Karas graduated from Paier School of Art in Connecticut and has since lived in Kansas City, New York, and now in Phoenix with his wife and two sons. He has had many different studios, including one in a sewing factory turned artist's co-op in New York, a sculptor's loft in a warehouse on Seattle's waterfront (the last house that Frank Lloyd Wright designed), and a small cottage on the grounds of an old desert lodge where he now works.

## SAVING SWEETNESS

When the little orphan, Sweetness, runs away from Mrs. Sump's orphanage, the sheriff sets off to find her before she runs into Coyote Pete, the meanest desperado in the West.

• • • • • • • • • • • • • • •

**"**I enjoyed the authentic Western flavor that Diane Stanley evoked in *Saving Sweetness*, and I wanted to complement that with authentic Western images. I looked out my window, I looked at my camera, and knew that the book would involve photographs. With a little of this and a little of that (and a lot of time in the dark room), I toned the photographs to integrate with the art.**"**

Book Title
*Saving Sweetness*

Author
**Diane Stanley**

Publisher
**G.P. Putnam's Sons**

Publication Date
**1996**

Illustration Medium
**Gouache, acrylic and pencil with toned cyanotype photographs**

# G. BRIAN KARAS

## TRUMAN'S AUNT FARM

Truman expects to receive an ant farm for his birthday. When he receives a farm of "aunts" instead, Truman trains them to be the best in the world.

• • • • • • • • • • • • • • •

"*Truman's Aunt Farm* is a lighthearted story about the friendship between Truman and his Aunt Fran. I wanted the artwork to be equally lighthearted, warm, fun, and uncomplicated."

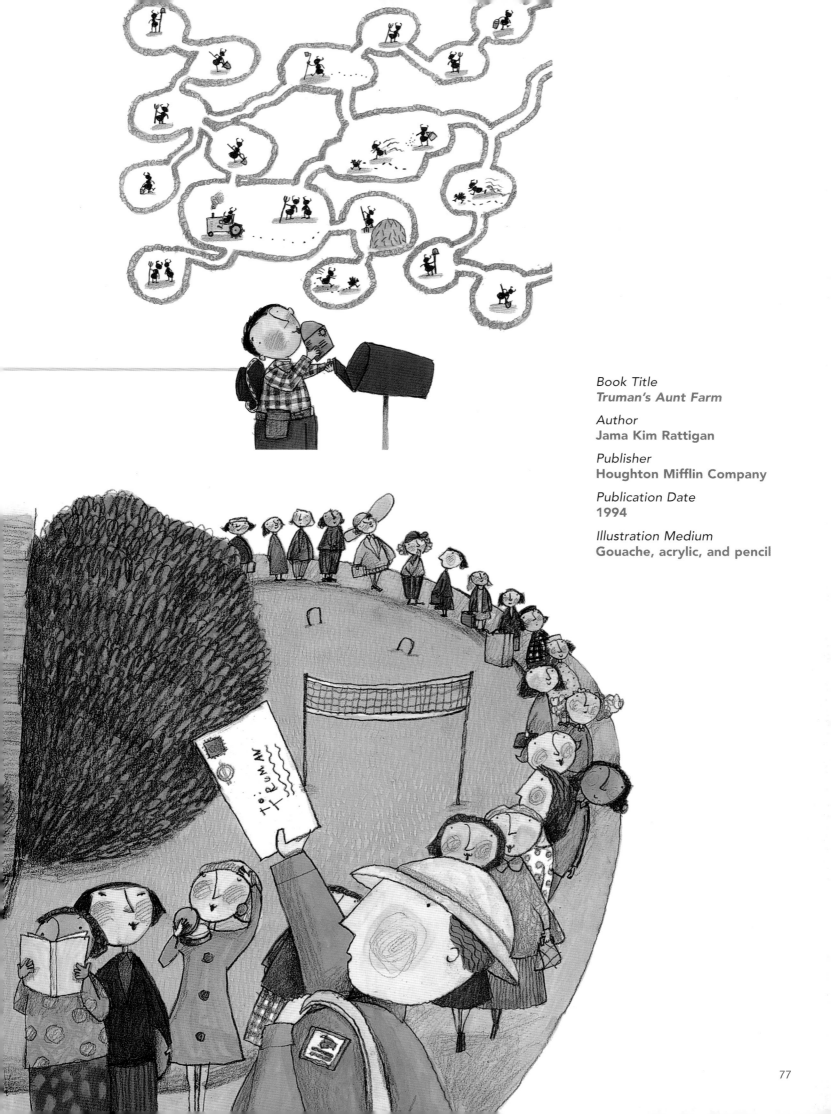

*Book Title*
***Truman's Aunt Farm***

*Author*
**Jama Kim Rattigan**

*Publisher*
**Houghton Mifflin Company**

*Publication Date*
**1994**

*Illustration Medium*
**Gouache, acrylic, and pencil**

# STEVEN KELLOGG

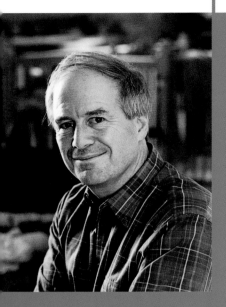

"I have loved picture books since childhood," Steven Kellogg says, "and took great pleasure during my early years in creating my own stories which I would recite, while scribbling accompanying illustrations for my two younger sisters". Determined to make art a major concentration in his life, Mr. Kellogg attended the Rhode Island School of Design on scholarship, where he majored in illustration. A fellowship sent him to Italy during his senior year, which proved to be "one of the most formative, sustaining, and enriching experiences" of his life. Since that time, he devoted himself to picture books, creating over ninety in the last thirty years. Mr. Kellogg hopes his books will encourage a lifetime association with pictures, words, and books.

## JACK AND THE BEANSTALK

This classic fairy tale describes the struggles of a youth to overcome his mother's cynicism and despair, and to prove his own mettle by confronting and outsmarting a brutish ogre.

• • • • • • • • • • • • • •

❝To retell and illustrate a classic fairy tale like *Jack and the Beanstalk*, I found it desirable and necessary to sink backward into the more remote, and in some cases, darker memories of my childhood. The story was a favorite of mine, and I tried to recapture the fear and fascination I felt in the presence of the sinister tall woman and the powerful ogre when I had first experienced the story in the guise of Jack. But I also tried to portray the evil pair as somewhat absurd in order to be true to the humor in Joseph Jacob's text, and also make the young hero's triumph more credible and fun.❞

*Book Title*
*Jack and the Beanstalk*

*Author*
**retold by Steven Kellogg**

*Publisher*
**Morrow Junior Books**

*Publication Date*
**1991**

*Illustration Medium*
**Watercolor, acrylics, colored ink,
colored pencil**

STEVEN KELLOGG

*Book Title*
**The Adventures of
Huckleberry Finn**

*Author*
**Mark Twain**

*Publisher*
**Morrow Junior Books**

*Publication Date*
**1994**

*Illustration Medium*
**Watercolor, acrylic,
colored ink, colored pencil**

# THE ADVENTURES OF HUCKLEBERRY FINN

Mark Twain's classic American story that interweaves the lives of an abused home-less boy and a runaway slave, and follows them on an epic raft voyage down the Mississippi River.

● ● ● ● ● ● ● ● ● ● ● ● ● ●

❝The paintings I did for *The Adventures of Huckleberry Finn* are larger than the reproductions in the book. Normally, I work in the same size as the book page in order to be in direct contact with the images as they will appear in relation to the typography and the reader's glance and touch. However, the fact that these paintings were not being done for a picture book, but for a monumental novel, demanded another approach. It was a privilege, a challenge, and a great pleasure to illustrate this icon of American literature, to select the incidents which would be highlighted by pictorial insights, and to be immersed for many months in the power, the beauty, and the humor of Mark Twain's magnificent writing.❞

# DANIEL KIRK

Daniel Kirk began his career as an art teacher some twenty-five years ago, only to leave the world of children aside for a long period of time as he pursued work in the "grown-up world of magazine illustration and advertising". With the birth of his first child, he was pulled back to using his talents to instruct and entertain children, and entered the world of illustrated picture books. Mr. Kirk has illustrated book covers, magazines, posters and CDs, and his work has been featured in numerous Society of Illustrators and AIGA shows. Mr. Kirk enjoys creating picture books, and hopes to continue to develop this talent for children for many years to come.

## THE DIGGERS
A steamshovel digs holes in the earth in preparation for train travel.

• • • • • • • • • • • • • • •

"This Margaret Wise Brown story was previously published in the early 1960s. . . but the text seems evocative of an even earlier era. I took it as my job to create new illustrations that recalled certain aspects of classic children's book illustrations from the 1930s-1950s. Since I didn't want it to look like an old book, however, I tried to give the artwork a more sophisticated, contemporary edge that brings more richness and personality to the work. The medium (oil on canvas) also brings a fine-art look to the illustrations, adding a further dimension of meaning."

*Book Title*
**Lucky's 24-Hour Garage**

*Author*
**Daniel Kirk**

*Publisher*
**Hyperion Books for Children**

*Publication Date*
**1996**

*Illustration Medium*
**Oil on canvas**

## LUCKY'S 24-HOUR GARAGE

In 1939, a gas station attendant works the night shift and takes care of customers who come to the station for help.

❝I spent a lot of time researching old photographs and illustrations to help me with my illustrations. I became quite fond of the look of the 1930s-1950s, and when I spotted an old gas station sign in an antique store, I was inspired to write a story about the activities surrounding a gas station in the 1930s. I hope the pictures in this book suggest something to the reader about the vitality of times past, making it seem real and contemporary without being simply nostalgic.❞

*Book Title*
**The Diggers**

*Author*
**Margaret Wise Brown**

*Publisher*
**Hyperion Books for Children**

*Publication Date*
**1995**

*Illustration Medium*
**Oil on canvas**

# JIM LaMARCHE

Jim LaMarche was born in Wausau, Wisconsin in 1952. His parents were both teachers, and he is the middle child in a family of five children. Mr. LaMarche grew up in the small town of Kewaskum—a beautiful area of lakes and rolling wooded hills with a river that ran through the town. He has been creating illustrations since 1976 and only recently devoted all his time to children's books. *The Rainbabies* won a number of awards including the Fiero di Bologna Graphic Prize, the American Bookseller's Book of the Year Award, and was a PBS Storytime Book. *The Carousel* was a featured Reading Rainbow Book.

*Book Title*
**The Rainbabies**

*Author*
**Laura Krauss Melmed**

*Publisher*
**Lothrop, Lee & Shepard Books**

*Publication Date*
**1992**

*Illustration Medium*
**Acrylic and colored pencil**

### THE RAINBABIES

A magic moonshower brings a childless couple a dozen tiny babies, who shower the couple with love and adventure. The old couple's kind care is rewarded in the end.

• • • • • • • • • • • • • •

**❝**I didn't want the pictures to have a 'once upon a time' look. I wanted to keep the possibility that this story took place maybe fifty years ago, maybe ten years ago, or maybe even yesterday. I was very lucky with *The Rainbabies*—lucky to be offered the story, lucky to find, right under my nose, the models I used. And lucky in the ease of the work, which seemed to have its own life and power. This book opened a lot of doors and possibilities for me. It will always have a very special place in my heart.**❞**

## GRANDMOTHER'S PIGEON

Grandmother is far more mysterious than anyone in her family knew, and now she has hitched a ride on a passing porpoise headed for Greenland. Her family sets out to understand her mysteries, including why there is a just-hatched nest of birds in Grandmother's bedroom.

• • • • • • • • • • • • • •

66 Since there is only one portrait of Grandmother in this Louise Erdrich story, the illustration needed to reveal a lot about this mysterious woman. In my drawing, Grandmother holds in her weathered, strong hands an ancient Chinese cup in which she brews a malodorous tea. She wears a worn blue jean jacket—perhaps she has just come in from cutting wood or training mules. Her hair is white and long, hinting that she's a little vain, but not fussy. Her wide-brimmed hat was perhaps given to her by a South American gaucho on one of her many adventures. The scarf she wears with a Parisian flair. 99

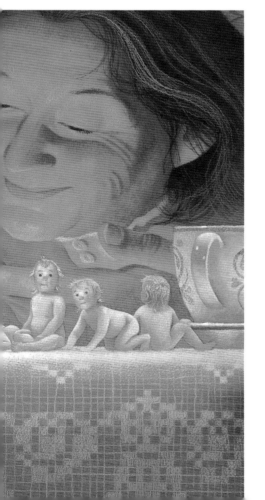

*Book Title*
**Grandmother's Pigeon**

*Author*
**Louise Erdrich**

*Publisher*
**Hyperion Books for Children**

*Publication Date*
**1996**

*Illustration Medium*
**Acrylic and colored pencil**

# JIM LaMARCHE

Book Title
*The Carousel*

Author
**Liz Rosenberg**

Publisher
**Harcourt Brace & Company**

Publication Date
**1995**

Illustration Medium
**Acrylic and colored pencil**

## THE CAROUSEL

Two sisters remember their mother telling them that carousel horses sleep all winter and wake in the spring. They soon discover the magic of living carousel horses and understand the lasting gift of their mother's love.

. . . . . . . . . . . . . . . .

❝In my drawings, I didn't see the carousel horses with fancy harnesses and bright jewels and colors. I wanted them stripped down to living, wild horses—a little dangerous. After they ran I wanted the reader to see the sweat and steam off their bodies. The two sisters have to contend with these wild horses, ultimately calming them and fixing the broken carousel machinery. For models I found real-life sisters with personalities that matched the story's sisters. The big sister is cautious and protective, the younger sister is impulsive and tough.❞

*Book Title*
**The Walloping Window-blind**

*Author*
**Charles E. Carryl**

*Publisher*
**Lothrop, Lee & Shepard Books**

*Publication Date*
**1993**

*Illustration Medium*
**Acrylic and pencil on watercolor paper**

## THE WALLOPING WINDOW-BLIND

An illustrated version of the nonsense poem about an extraordinary ship and the misadventures of her madcap crew.

. . . . . . . . . . . . . . . .

❝In *The Walloping Window-blind*, I used my sons and the neighborhood gang of wild things as my models. They brought an instant energy and extra life to my drawings. My middle son posed for the cookie eating, comic reading first mate. Besides asking for his regular modeling fee, he was allowed to dunk, drip and eat half a bag of oreo cookies in bed as I sketched him.❞

# TED LEWIN

Ted Lewin's first memory of
drawing is from a metal-armed
copying toy he received for
Christmas and a "magic pad,"
on which he could pull up a
flap and make whatever was
drawn disapppear. Mr. Lewin
grew up in upstate New York.
In order to help pay expenses
as a student at the Pratt
Institute in Brooklyn, he
began a secondary career in
professional wrestling. By the
late 1960s, Mr. Lewin
obtained work illustrating
children's books, and today, he
often relies on his knowledge
of and concern for wildlife
and their habitats throughout
the world when illustrating
books.Mr. Lewin is the
recipient of the Caldecott
Honor Award, 1994, for *Peppe
the Lamplighter*.

*Book Title*
**The Day of Ahmed's Secret**

*Author*
**Florence Heide and Judith Gilliland**

*Publisher*
**Lothrop, Lee & Shepard Books**

*Publication Date*
**1990**

*Illustration Medium*
**Watercolor**

# THE DAY OF AHMED'S SECRET

A boy delivers bottled gas in Cairo to help support his family. His secret is that he has learned to write his name.

• • • • • • • • • • • • • • •

66Setting the scene in Cairo was a great challenge. I had never been there, so the authors gave me a tremendous amount of visual material. They even sent out people to photograph certain details I needed. I wanted to show Ahmed going about his busy schedule, helping his family, and always surrounded by this bustling city. I made the final scenes dark to enhance the drama of his secret.99

*Book Title*
**Amazon Boy**

*Author*
**Ted Lewin**

*Publisher*
**Simon & Schuster Books
for Young Readers**

*Publication Date*
**1993**

*Illustration Medium*
**Watercolor**

## AMAZON BOY

A boy travels down the Amazon with his father to Belem where he learns of the bounty of the river and how it is threatened. Returning home, he catches a big fish and decides to release it.

• • • • • • • • • • • • • •

66*Amazon Boy* grew out of a trip I made to Brazil and the Amazon. I wanted to take the reader from the vast, primal rainforest downriver by steamer to the bustling market in Belem. The dark night riverboat spread evokes Paulo's dark dreams. I took 150 rolls of film on my trip, and drew on them for a sense of place. I had seen men carrying great fish on their heads, which I recreated in the book.99

*Book Title*
**Peppe the Lamplighter**

*Author*
**Elisa Bartone**

*Publisher*
**Lothrop, Lee & Shepard Books**

*Publication Date*
**1993**

*Illustration Medium*
**Watercolor**

## PEPPE THE LAMPLIGHTER

A boy in Little Italy (circa 1890) gets a job lighting the gas lamps, to the disdain of his father.

• • • • • • • • • • • • •

66The book takes place before the advent of electricity. The main challenge was to illuminate the darkness. On the cover, I set the mood of the whole book: a deep void of blackness with Peppe bringing the light. The concept of the story has a dark side as well—the father's strong criticism and disapproval of Peppe, which are reinforced in the dark pictures.99

# E.B. LEWIS

E.B. Lewis was born and educated in Philadelphia, Pennsylvania. Inspired by two uncles who were artists, Mr. Lewis has been studying art since he was a child. At Temple University's Tyler School of Art, he discovered his medium of preference—watercolor. His work has become part of major private collections and is displayed in galleries throughout the United States. Mr. Lewis says of his work, "Painting captures a moment of feeling and holds it for us to remember. Painting documents life, and that's what I do".

*Book Title*
**Down the Road**

*Author*
**Alice Schertle**

*Publisher*
**Harcourt Brace & Company**

*Publication Date*
**1995**

*Illustration Medium*
**Watercolor**

## DOWN THE ROAD

Hetty is very careful with the eggs she has bought on her very first trip to the store, but she runs into trouble when she stops to pick apples.

• • • • • • • • • • • • • • • •

66More than any book I've done so far, the illustrations in *Down the Road* are the closest examples to my fine-art work. It was a great vehicle to display watercolor at its best. Light, shadow, and the translucency of the medium allow the creation of an atmosphere that no other medium conveys. To really like the story influences my work and this classic American tale is one of my favorites.99

# E.B. LEWIS

*Book Title*
**Fire on the Mountain**

*Author*
**Jane Kurtz**

*Publisher*
**Simon & Schuster Books
for Young Readers**

*Publication Date*
**1994**

*Illustration Medium*
**Watercolor**

# FIRE ON THE MOUNTAIN

A clever young shepherd boy uses his wits to gain a fortune for himself and his sister from a haughty witch.

• • • • • • • • • • • • • •

**"***Fire on the Mountain* has a special place in my heart. It represents my first accomplishment in the category of children's book illustration. For me it had all the excitement of a trip to a foreign land. I believe this is an important element in children's books—to be able to travel in your mind through reading. My approach was to make the book as authentic as possible, conveying all the flavor of Ethiopia. The success of the art-work is measured by Ethiopians who have viewed the book and were surprised to find out I had not yet traveled there.**"**

Fred Marcellino was born in New York City, where he resides today. He studied at Cooper Union, the Yale University School of Art, and in Venice, Italy, under a Fulbright study grant. Before illustrating children's books he designed numerous book jackets, many of which won prizes, including three National Book awards. Mr. Marcellino won an honorable mention for the Critici in Erba Prize at The Bologna Book Fair for *The Steadfast Tin Soldier* and received the Caldecott Honor Award, 1991 for his first picture book, *Puss In Boots.*

*Book Title*
**Puss in Boots**

*Author*
**Charles Perrault, translated by
Malcolm Arthur**

*Publisher*
**Farrar, Straus & Giroux, Inc.**

*Publication Date*
**1990**

*Illustration Medium*
**Colored pencils**

## PUSS IN BOOTS

*Puss in Boots* was written in 1697. The story's inexperienced young hero achieves wealth, position, and even the love of a princess; all with the help of his alter ego, the sly and resourceful Puss. Being a cat, Puss can literally get away with murder, at least when his victim is a mouse.

• • • • • • • • • • • • • •

**"**Since *Puss in Boots* is so famous, and has been illustrated so often and at least in the case of Gustave Doré, so well, it posed a wonderful challenge as a first picture book. The tale's fame, I think, is justly deserved, and, like a great opera or play, it can always stand new interpretation. The boisterous humor and the extraordinary character of Puss were my stepping stones into the work. During a European vacation, a side trip to Fountainbleau was an extra inspiration. The book is illustrated in colored pencils, a medium which is both intricate and crude, allowing for richness in detail, without the option or danger of overrefinement.**"**

Emily Arnold McCully has enjoyed drawing since childhood. After graduating from Brown University, Ms. McCully worked in advertising and publishing, eventually compiling a portfolio of illustrations. She found that her playwriting and acting background was very helpful in telling stories with pictures. As she gradually obtained more assignments to illustrate book covers and advertisements, she also nurtured her love of writing. Ms. McCully eventually published two novels, and today is the recipient of the O. Henry Award in fiction. Ms. McCully is also the recipient of the Christopher Award and the Biennale at Bratislava for *Picnic*, and the Caldecott Award and *The New York Times* Best Illustrated Award, 1992 for *Mirette on the High Wire*.

## MIRETTE ON THE HIGH WIRE

The story of a young girl in Paris and a high wire walker who has become paralyzed by fear.

. . . . . . . . . . . . . .

❝When I proposed *Mirette On the High Wire*, the art director observed that paintings would evoke Paris in the 1890s more than drawings would. Painterliness was added to the mix. Mirette and its successors have represented my attempt to teach myself to paint, and to be more realistic in my observations of the world. The movies in my head are no longer comedies, but dramas. I aim, too, for historical accuracy and to bring the reader into the action by making the pictures as energetic as possible.❞

Book Title
*Picnic*

Author
**Emily Arnold McCully**

Publisher
**HarperCollins Publishers**

Publication Date
**1984**

Illustration Medium
**Pen and watercolor**

# PICNIC

After a large family of mice embarks on a picnic, the smallest mouse falls unnoticed from the truck and copes with being lost but not missed. Finally, it is missed, and found.

• • • • • • • • • • • • • • •

"I did not realize, at first, that words were unneccessary for this tale. The pictures were carefully worked out so that the story could be followed with visual clues. I used the landscape near my country home and, after some hesitation, let the mice be big enough to inhabit it. They are all drawn so as to display fully human emotions and individuality, but with simplicity."

Book Title
**Mirette on the High Wire**

Author
**Emily Arnold McCully**

Publisher
**G.P. Putnam's Sons**

Publication Date
**1992**

Illustration Medium
**Watercolor with pastel highlights**

## STARRING MIRETTE AND BELLINI

Mirette and Bellini are a renowned high wire act. Invited to cross the frozen Neva in St. Petersburg, Mirette sees the haunted faces of starving peasants. She demands an explanation and makes a public call for freedom.

• • • • • • • • • • • • • • •

❝I wanted Mirette to be struck by suffering in the world and for the art to show the contrast between the way the poor and the rich lived at the turn of the century. St. Petersburg offered the right setting for that, but produced the challenge of depicting classical architecture on a horizontal plain.❞

*Book Title*
**The Pirate Queen**

*Author*
**Emily Arnold McCully**

*Publisher*
**G.P. Putnam's Sons**

*Publication Date*
**1995**

*Illustration Medium*
**Watercolor and pastel**

# THE PIRATE QUEEN
The story of a real-life Renaissance woman pirate.

● ● ● ● ● ● ● ● ● ● ● ● ● ● ●

❝I use watercolor because it permits speed of execution and the accidents are stimulating. With *The Pirate Queen*, I was persuaded that seascapes would be as dramatic as action scenes, so I allowed the paint to do more of the work than usual, letting washes create waves and mists. Nearly all my books tell the story of a persevering, brave, interesting girl or woman in an historical setting. I am redressing the imbalance of my own early reading, which was all about boys' adventures—there was so little about girls to feed my appetite. Many long for stories reflecting their own sense of independence and adventure. Today's boys will read about girls if the characters are interesting enough.❞

*Book Title*
**Starring Mirette and Bellini**

*Author*
**Emily Arnold McCully**

*Publisher*
**G.P. Putnam's Sons**

*Publication Date*
**1997**

*Illustration Medium*
**Watercolor and pastel**

# MICHAEL McCURDY

Michael McCurdy was born in New York City in 1942. He began drawing pictures as a child and later completed a Bachelor of Fine Arts at the School of the Museum of Fine Arts in Boston. He received his Master of Fine Arts from Tufts University in Medford. In 1965, he began his freelance illustration career and later became a printer and publisher of new poetry and fiction writing. In addition to being the illustrator of over 100 books, Mr. McCurdy was the publisher of Penmaen Press Books. He has also taught at the School of the Museum of Fine Arts in Boston, Concord Academy, and Wellesley College. Today, the artist lives in the Berkshire Hills of Massachusetts, where he enjoys the woodlands and open fields that are portrayed so dramatically in his scratch-board drawings.

## LUCY'S CHRISTMAS

In the fall of 1909 in rural New England—a time and place when the arrival of a new stove from the Sears Roebuck catalogue was an extraordinary event—a young girl gets an early start on making Christmas presents for her family and friends, which they will open at the church's Christmas event.

• • • • • • • • • • • • • • •

66Many of the drawings for *Lucy's Christmas* had to be revised. For one thing, I had included cats and dogs in the drawings which were carefully deleted because of the author's concern that no animals had ever been admitted into his mother Lucy's farmhouse. The house depicted is Lucy's actual house, as are the room and the Glenwood stove. I did the drawings in black-and-white scratchboard and then made copies which were hand painted in watercolor.99

*Book Title*
**The Beasts of Bethlehem**

*Author*
**X. J. Kennedy**

*Publisher*
**Margaret K. McElderry Books**

*Publication Date*
**1992**

*Illustration Medium*
**Scratchboard**

# THE BEASTS OF BETHLEHEM

Nineteen poems, each in the voice of a creature that was present in the stable at the time of Christ's birth.

• • • • • • • • • • • • • • •

66 *The Beasts of Bethlehem* was a collaboration between old friends. The poet Kennedy was a teacher of mine at college whom I approached about doing a book together consisting of animal poems. He suggested the nativity theme. Fitting the variety of animal shapes—from a mosquito to an ox—into one uniform vertical shape was the major challenge. I used scratchboard, made copies, and then hand colored them using watercolor paints. 99

*Book Title*
**Lucy's Christmas**

*Author*
**Donald Hall**

*Publisher*
**Harcourt Brace & Company**

*Publication Date*
**1994**

*Illustration Medium*
**Scratchboard**

# MICHAEL McCURDY

## GIANTS IN THE LAND

A history of logging the king's forests in pre-revolutionary New England.

• • • • • • • • • • • • • •

"As a book artist, my images bubble up through the act of reading a manuscript. Of course, practical considerations have to be addressed as well, such as a book's length and content. I have illustrated books using either the medium of wood engraving or the technique of scratch-board. Sometimes color is added, but the power of black and white lent itself nicely to the rugged imagery of *Giants in the Land*."

# THE GETTYSBURG ADDRESS

Four months after the famous Battle of Gettysburg, Abraham Lincoln delivered a speech at the battleground as part of the commemoration of a national cemetery. The date was November, 1863.

• • • • • • • • • • • • • • •

66*The Gettysburg Address* developed through my interest in Abraham Lincoln and the Civil War, and the fact that I had a great-grandfather who fought at Gettysburg and lived to tell the tale. The speech is so abstract that I had difficulty conjuring up images for certain phrases. I believe that the black-and-white scratchboard drawings were well suited to the drama of the speech. The type was set by hand, most unusual for any commercial book done today.99

*Book Title*
***The Gettysburg Address***

*Author*
**Abraham Lincoln**

*Publisher*
**Houghton Mifflin Company**

*Publication Date*
**1995**

*Illustration Medium*
**Scratchboard**

*Book Title*
***Giants in the Land***

*Author*
**Diana Appelbaum**

*Publisher*
**Houghton Mifflin Company**

*Publication Date*
**1993**

*Illustration Medium*
**Scratchboard**

# SUSAN MEDDAUGH

Susan Meddaugh's hands-on education began at Houghton Mifflin Company where she worked for ten years as a design and art director in the children's book department. Ms. Meddaugh left the publisher to pursue her freelance career, which led to a variety of illustrations for *The New Boston Review* and *The Boston Globe*, as well as various educational publishers. "My main love," she declares, "has been trade picture books and I have been fortunate enough to be able to illustrate fifteen books for other authors, as well as nine books of my own". Ms. Meddaugh is the recipient of *The New York Times* Best Illustrated Book Award, 1992, State Young Readers Awards in several states including Pennsylvania and Nebraska, and numerous starred reviews for *Martha Speaks*.

*Book Title*
**Hog-Eye**

*Author*
**Susan Meddaugh**

*Publisher*
**Houghton Mifflin Company**

*Publication Date*
**1995**

*Illustration Medium*
**Watercolor, pen and ink**

## HOG-EYE

A small pig misses the hated school bus, and must explain to her skeptical family why she never got to school. Her creative tale of getting on the wrong bus, meeting and outwitting a wolf is greeted with some disbelief, yet enables her to discover her talent for storytelling.

· · · · · · · · · · · · · · ·

**❝**I remember, as a child, being tremendously worried about getting on the right bus and getting off at the right spot! Years later, I saw my son and his most confident elementary school friends having their own set of anxieties about the school bus. So, this was the beginning of a tale dealing with big yellow bus nightmares. It became, as well, the story of a child coping with the problem, and in the process, discovering her talent. The challenges were to say everything I wanted to say within 32 pages, and to visually separate what the girl was saying from her family's reactions.**❞**

# SUSAN MEDDAUGH

## MARTHA CALLING

Further adventures of Martha the dog who talks as she discovers the joys of the telephone and the injustice of the words: 'no dogs allowed'.

• • • • • • • • • • • • • • •

"As with all my books, I want to tell a good story through a combination of words and pictures. I hope for humor. The expressiveness of the characters may be what I most enjoy doing. To this end, pen and ink work for me. I rely on 'visual inspirations'. . . which tell more about the character than ten pages of text. My ongoing challenge is to maintain some control and consistency while conveying a feeling of spontaneity in my illustrations—a quality often found in early sketches and often lost in final art."

*Book Title*
**Martha Calling**

*Author*
**Susan Meddaugh**

*Publisher*
**Houghton Mifflin Company**

*Publication Date*
**1994**

*Illustration Medium*
**Watercolor, pen and ink**

*Book Title*
**Martha Speaks**

*Author*
**Susan Meddaugh**

*Publisher*
**Houghton Mifflin Company**

*Publication Date*
**1992**

*Illustration Medium*
**Watercolor, pen and ink**

## MARTHA SPEAKS

Martha the dog eats alphabet soup. The letters go up to her brain instead of down to her stomach, and Martha speaks. And speaks. And speaks.

• • • • • • • • • • • • • • •

❝When I'm doing my own books, there is no separation of art and text. They come to me together, and they tell the story together. When my son was in first grade, he jokingly asked me: 'If Martha (our dog) ate alphabet soup, would she be able to talk?' An image popped into my head when he asked me this question, and it's the perfect example of words and pictures happening at the same time. The function of the art is to help tell the story through character, expression, and, I hope, humor.❞

# PAUL MORIN

Paul Morin's immersion in the culture, people, music, and sounds of varied countries are reflected in his illustrations of world folktales and myths. Mr. Morin has lectured at conferences, schools, and libraries across the country on his art, music, and on primitive cultures. With a freelance career that has spanned the past sixteen years, Mr. Morin's work has been featured by advertising agencies and publishers across North America, and exhibited at The International Opera Festival, Imperial Life, and the Museum of Civilization. His awards include the Canadian Library Association Book of the Year in 1991 and 1992, the International Board on Books for Young People Award in 1992, and the Society of Illustrators Award in 1993.

*Book Title*
**The Mud Family**

*Author*
**Betsy James**

*Publisher*
**G.P. Putnam's Sons**

*Publication Date*
**1994**

*Illustration Medium*
**Alkyds, mixed media**

## THE MUD FAMILY

A girl creates a mud family when drought begins to threaten the Anasazi's way of life. Through a magic rain dance, she saves the family and is reunited with her real family.

• • • • • • • • • • • • •

"I began work on *The Mud Family* by visiting the Southwest for location research. I travelled throughout the Four Corners, and visited dozens of Anasazi ruins. . . . One morning in Southern Utah, I hiked to a cliff dwelling and arrived just before sunrise. As the light increased, I glanced up at the rock wall behind the complex. There, amongst many adult red ochre handprints, was the handprint of a small child. Just then, sunlight beamed in the alcove, and at that instant, I felt truly inspired towards *The Mud Family*. When I returned home, before I began work on the paintings, I transformed the walls in my living room into a textured cliff with some 1,200 petroglyphs on it."

# PAUL MORIN

## THE ORPHAN BOY

When Kileken, the orphan boy, mysteriously appears, an old man who had always longed for a child is delighted. When the old man discovers Kileken's special powers, he becomes desperate to know the boy's magic.

• • • • • • • • • • • • • • •

"I set out for the Great Rift Valley in East Africa to do research for *The Orphan Boy*. There, the Maasai people still live a simple (and complex) life among the spectacular backdrop of the African Savannah. The magical feelings I felt from the Maasai and the passion which I incorporated into the paintings were a new branch on my creative path. The journey showed me that if I can observe and absorb experiences, I can be in a better position to translate those experiences into images. I feel that the book depicts a proud people and gives us insight into their mythology, which is also our mythology."

Book Title
*The Dragon's Pearl*

Author
**Julie Lawson**

Publisher
**Clarion Books**

Publication Date
**1993**

Illustration Medium
**Alkyds, mixed media**

Book Title
*The Orphan Boy*

Author
**Tololwa Mollel**

Publisher
**Clarion Books**

Publication Date
**1990**

Illustration Medium
**Alkyds, mixed media, assemblage**

## THE DRAGON'S PEARL

A Chinese folk story of a boy who finds a magic pearl which brings his family good fortune, and transforms him into a dragon.

• • • • • • • • • • • • • • •

**“**Traditional cultures are of profound interest to me, grounded as they are in the importance of spirit, earth, harmony and wisdom.**”**

113

# MATT NOVAK

*Book Title*
**Elmer Blunt's Open House**

*Author*
**Matt Novak**

*Publisher*
**Orchard Books**

*Publication Date*
**1992**

*Illustration Medium*
**Watercolor and colored pencil**

Matt Novak grew up in the small town of Sheppton, Pennsylvania. As a child he put on puppet shows for his classmates, made animated films, and drew and painted constantly. Later in life he studied for his Bachelor of Fine Arts at the School of Visual Arts in New York City, where writing and illustrating books for children captured his imagination. He has worked as a puppeteer, teacher, and Disney artist. *Mouse TV* is a *School Library Journal* Best Book and a Parents' Choice Honor Award winner 1994. Mr. Novak's illustrations have appeared in the Original Art Exhibition as well as many other museums and galleries.

# ELMER BLUNT'S OPEN HOUSE

Several animals and a robber explore Elmer Blunt's home when he forgets to close the door on his way to work.

• • • • • • • • • • • • • •

"I wanted this book to have a million surprises in it, so the reader will continually find something new. The challenge was to look at everyday objects through the eyes of animals who had never seen a teacup or a refrigerator before. This is a very active story, and I felt that colored pencils would best capture this energetic feeling."

# MATT NOVAK

Book Title
**Mouse TV**

Author
**Matt Novak**

Publisher
**Orchard Books**

Publication Date
**1994**

Illustration Medium
**Acrylic paint on paper**

## MOUSE TV

Each member of the mouse family wants to watch something different on television, but they discover a solution to their problem one night when the television does not work.

• • • • • • • • • • • • • •

**"**This is probably the most complicated book I have done to date. Each page is almost a story unto itself, and I had to make sure that the overall story did not get bogged down in the details. So, I made the mouse family freestanding on the page to help carry their own story along and separate them from the individual images on the boxy television screens. I used acrylic paints because they are so perfect for capturing the tiny details which fill this book.**"**

Marjorie Priceman studied art at the Rhode Island School of Design. After graduating, she held a variety of jobs including graphic designer, textile designer, and fashion illustrator, as well as illustrator for a variety of magazines and newspapers. Ms. Priceman wrote and illustrated her first picture book in 1989—*Friend or Frog*. Since then, she has illustrated fifteen books including *Zin! Zin! Zin! A Violin* which is an American Library Association Notable Book, a Reading Rainbow feature selection, a Storytime feature selection, winner of *The New York Times* Best Illustrated Book Award, 1995, and the Caldecott Honor Award, 1996.

## COUSIN RUTH'S TOOTH

A sequel to *Rachel Fister's Blister*, the story of Cousin Ruth who lost a tooth and the suggestions and prescriptions of the extended Fister family to find it or replace it.

• • • • • • • • • • • • • •

66As this story is a sequel, the style and medium were predetermined. I tried to create chaotic, frenzied, hopefully humorous illustrations that would fit the funny, fast-paced rhyme of the text. The adults were given a caricatured treatment to match their absurd suggestions and actions.99

*Book Title*
*Cousin Ruth's Tooth*

*Author*
**Amy MacDonald**

*Publisher*
**Houghton Mifflin Company**

*Publication Date*
**1996**

*Illustration Medium*
**Watercolor**

*Book Title*
*Zin! Zin! Zin! A Violin*

*Author*
**Lloyd Moss**

*Publisher*
**Simon & Schuster Books for Young Readers**

*Publication Date*
**1995**

*Illustration Medium*
**Gouache**

# ZIN! ZIN! ZIN! A VIOLIN

A counting book which introduces the various musicians and musical instruments in an orchestra.

· · · · · · · · · · · · · · · ·

**❝**I attempted to create a visual expression of music through curving compositions, free-flowing backgrounds, looping arms and legs of the musicians. I gave the players characteristics in common with their instruments such as the trumpeter's dress which flares like a trumpet, and the flutist who wears a slim column of a dress with buttons down the front. The cats, mouse, and dog were added as a visual subplot to entertain younger readers and as a compromise to a suggestion from the publisher to have animal musicians. This proved problematic since animals don't have the opposable thumbs necessary to correctly grip the instruments. The book's first purpose, moreover, is to instruct. I used gouache diluted with water to make amorphous, undulating rhythmic backgrounds and foreground figures painted in bolder, opaque colors to act almost like 'notes' floating over a sheet of music.**❞**

# VLADIMIR RADUNSKY

Vladimir Radunsky was born in Russia in 1954. In 1982, he came to the United States and settled in New York City where he designed art books for various publishers. In 1995, the Children's Television Workshop invited Mr. Radunsky to create an animated short film based on the art from *The Maestro Plays*. The film was shown on Sesame Street, and internationally syndicated on PBS. Reading Rainbow has featured *Hail to Mail* in its 1995 programming, also syndicated on PBS. Mr. Radunsky's books have been translated into many languages and sold in Germany, France, Britain, Spain, Australia, New Zealand, and Japan. His work has been exhibited in galleries and museums throughout the world.

## TELEPHONE

From doves wanting gloves to baboons needing spoons, animal after animal calls on the telephone until the harried, hapless hero of this classic Russian nonsense poem is at his wits' end.

• • • • • • • • • • • • • •

"My artwork is composed of mixed media. As my publisher so well describes, the collages 'are made with several different types of paper painted with acrylics, color photocopies of images from magazines, some string and some feathers.'"

Book Title
*Telephone*

Author
**Jamey Gambrell**

Publisher
**North-South Books Inc.**

Publication Date
**1996**

Illustration Medium
**Collage**

## THE MAESTRO PLAYS

Humorous rhymes accompany pictures of the antics and sounds of a musician's recital.

· · · · · · · · · · · · · · · ·

**"**I don't pick the medium I work in, but rather, it just happens. And most of the elements I use are repeated in various combinations. Recently, I came across a story by Hans Christian Andersen. In it, I found this thought that pretty closely resembles my work principle: 'Ah. . . Godfather could really tell fairy tales—they were long and plentiful. And at Christmas time he would take a thick, blank album and paste in it pictures that he cut out of books and newspapers. When he could not find a picture that fit the story, he could draw one.'**"**

*Book Title*
**The Maestro Plays**

*Author*
**Bill Martin Jr.**

*Publisher*
**Harcourt Brace & Company**

*Publication Date*
**1994**

*Illustration Medium*
**Collage**

# JAMES E. RANSOME

Book Title
*Uncle Jed's Barbershop*

Author
**Margaree King Mitchell**

Publisher
**Simon & Schuster Books for Young Readers**

Publication Date
**1993**

Illustration Medium
**Oil on paper**

The roots of James E. Ransome's creative talents began as a young child in the small town of Rich Square, North Carolina. "Living in the rural South did not provide many opportunities for the formal study of art, so I eventually began creating my own stories, usually focusing on the invented and real-life adventures of my friends". Mr. Ransome learned the elements of visual storytelling through classes in filmmaking and photography at Bergenfield High School. He later graduated from Pratt Institute with a Bachelor of Fine Arts degree in illustration and continued to study painting and drawing at the Art Students League in New York City. *Uncle Jed's Barber Shop* won a Coretta Scott King Honor Book Award and is an American Library Association Notable Book. His work is featured in the permanent children's book art collection of North Carolina's Charlotte Library.

## UNCLE JED'S BARBERSHOP

Despite serious obstacles and setbacks, Sarah Jean's Uncle Jed, the only black barber in the county, pursues his dream of saving enough money to open his own barbershop.

● ● ● ● ● ● ● ● ● ● ● ● ● ● ●

❝I wanted to convey a sense of strong family ties and emotional bonds while portraying the rich and natural beauty of the South. The colors of oil paints possess a heavy, rich quality which was needed in order to paint the earth tones used throughout the book. My hope was that the reader would come away from the story with a truer sense of character and respect for the daily struggles which confronted Uncle Jed.❞

# JAMES E. RANSOME

*Book Title*
**The Wagon**

*Author*
**Tony Johnston**

*Publisher*
**Tambourine Books**

*Publication Date*
**1996**

*Illustration Medium*
**Oil on paper**

## THE WAGON

A young boy is sustained by his family as he endures the difficulties of being a slave, but when he finally gains his freedom, his joy is tempered by the death of President Lincoln.

• • • • • • • • • • • • • • •

"*The Wagon* is my most complete book dealing with slavery. I felt it was important to show that slaves were men, women, children, and grandparents—people that laughed, cried, loved, and created. It is now time to create images that focus on the strength of these people. I set out to show a family that loved and cared for each other in the midst of a harsh and dangerous environment. The father, as master craftsman, not only cuts down the tree for the wagon, but shapes it into a working piece of art. With the simplest of tools, he shapes the smooth, dark wood into a chariot that will one day carry them to freedom."

# CELIE AND THE HARVEST FIDDLER

Celie, a young African American girl living in the South in the 1870s, wants desperately to win the costume contest at the All Hallow's Eve harvest festival.

. . . . . . . . . . . . . . . . .

66 The Africans that were brought to the United States and forced to work on plantations, brought with them beliefs in magic, spirits, conjuring, and the medicinal power of roots. . . . The authors cleverly chose Halloween night, when we celebrate the supernatural, as the setting for the story of a mysterious fiddler who is rumored to quietly slip in and out of towns to excite crowds with his playing. With my desire to explore this belief in the spirit world combined with my love of the work of Toni Morrison and other African American writers (who weave myth and mysticism into their stories of black life in America), I gladly accepted the challenge of illustrating this story. 99

Book Title
*Celie and the Harvest Fiddler*

Authors
**Vanessa and Valerie Flournoy**

Publisher
**Tambourine Books**

Publication Date
**1995**

Illustration Medium
**Oil on paper**

Peggy Rathmann grew up in the suburbs of St. Paul, Minnesota. She earned a Bachelor of Arts in psychology from the University of Minnesota, studied commercial art at the American Academy in Chicago, and fine art at the Atelier Lack in Minneapolis, Minnesota. During classes at the Otis Parsons School of Design in Los Angeles, Ms. Rathmann wrote and illustrated her first three published books. The second, *Good Night, Gorilla*, is a 1995 American Library Association Notable Book, and the third, *Officer Buckle and Gloria*, is a Caldecott Award winner, 1996.

## GOOD NIGHT, GORILLA

The story of a young gorilla who borrows a sleepy zookeeper's keys, then leads a parade of animals home to the zookeeper's bedroom.

• • • • • • • • • • • • • • •

❝When I was little, the highlight of the summer was running barefoot through the grass, in the dark, screaming. We played kick-the-can, and three-times-around-the-house. Sometimes, we just stood staring into other people's picture windows, wondering what it would be like to go home to someone else's house. These childhood memories inspired *Good Night Gorilla*, which I created as a wordless story.❞

*Book Title*
**Bootsie Barker Bites**

*Author*
**Barbara Bottner**

*Publisher*
**G.P. Putnam's Sons**

*Publication Date*
**1992**

*Illustration Medium*
**Watercolor and ink**

## BOOTSIE BARKER BITES

The story of a child forced to deal with the unpleasant daughter of her mother's best friend.

● ● ● ● ● ● ● ● ● ● ● ● ●

**❝**I used my own face as a model for Bootsie. Since Bootsie Barker is a psychopath with no redeeming qualities whatsoever, I was afraid if I used anybody else's face, that person and every other person who looked like the character would be offended. So I dug out my school picture from the fourth grade (I was a tense child with clenched teeth and a protruding jaw) and transformed it into Bootsie.**❞**

*Book Title*
**Good Night, Gorilla**

*Author*
**Peggy Rathmann**

*Publisher*
**G.P. Putnam's Sons**

*Publication Date*
**1994**

*Illustration Medium*
**Watercolor, colored pencil, and black ink**

PEGGY RATHMANN

Book Title
**Officer Buckle and Gloria**

Author
**Peggy Rathmann**

Publisher
**G.P. Putnam's Sons**

Publication Date
**1995**

Illustration Medium
**Watercolor and black ink**

## OFFICER BUCKLE AND GLORIA

The story of an earnest school safety officer whose lectures improve after he is assigned to the canine unit. Officer Buckle doesn't realize his sudden popularity stems from the heroic efforts of his police dog, Gloria, who acts out the safety tips behind Buckle's back.

• • • • • • • • • • • • • • •

66We have a videotape of my mother chatting in the dining room while, unnoticed by her or the cameraman, the dog is licking every poached egg on the buffet. The next scene shows the whole family at the breakfast table, complimenting my mother on the delicious poached eggs. The dog, of course, is pretending not to know what a poached egg is. The first time we watched the tape we were so shocked, we couldn't stop laughing. I suspect that videotape had a big influence on my choice of subject matter in *Officer Buckle and Gloria*.99

Barry Root was born in Huntsville, Alabama and grew up in Decatur, Georgia. He was educated at the Ringling School of Art in Sarasota, Florida. In 1980, Mr. Root moved to New York. There he began illustrating for various magazines, newspapers and advertisements, and created his first picture book—*The Araboolies of Liberty Street*. He now lives in rural Lancaster County, Pennsylvania with his wife, Kimberly (also an illustrator), their two children, and "a couple of good-for-nothing dogs".

## THE ARABOOLIES OF LIBERTY STREET

The General and Mrs. Pinch don't want the children of Liberty Street to have any fun, and when the Araboolies move in with their many pets, the Pinches are outraged.

• • • • • • • • • • • • • •

❝*The Araboolies of Liberty Street* was my first book and so everything about it was a challenge. The most important step was developing the characters, their pets and vehicle. I requested changes in the text to accommodate my ideas, especially color schemes. I had a lot of fun inventing the strange animals the Araboolies kept as pets. The book dictated a large cast of characters, with children, animals, toys, and furniture crowding every page. This fact, combined with my layered painting technique, kept me busy with this book for many months.❞

Book Title
*The Araboolies of Liberty Street*

Author
**Sam Swope**

Publisher
**Crown Publishers, Inc.**

Publication Date
**1989**

Illustration Medium
**Watercolor and gouache**

Kimberly Bulcken Root was born in York, Pennsylvania and grew up in Connecticut and South Carolina. In 1979, she graduated from the Parsons School of Design. Ms. Root began her career creating line art and black-and-white illustrations for *The New York Times*, *The Village Voice*, and *The Boston Globe* among other magazines and newspapers. Ms. Root has illustrated fourteen books for children, and was awarded the silver medal in the Children's Book Original Art Exhibition from The Society of Illustrators for *Papa's Bedtime Story* in 1993.

*Book Title*
**Papa's Bedtime Story**

*Author*
**Mary Lee Donovan**

*Publisher*
**Alfred A. Knopf, Inc.**

*Publication Date*
**1993**

*Illustration Medium*
**Pen, ink, and watercolor**

## PAPA'S BEDTIME STORY

A human father begins a bedtime story to his child and animal fathers pick up the tale until it runs full circle. The story occurs during a warm June night beginning with a thunderstorm and ending with tree frogs singing after the rain.

• • • • • • • • • • • • • • •

**"**In *Papa's Bedtime Story*, the warm and loving relationship between fathers and their babies is important, and I tried to show this through gestures of the characters—mainly the papas hugging the babies. The cycle of the story is also important and I tried to show this by echoing shapes and motifs from one page to the next. For example, a crack in a wall might resemble a tree on the next page, or swirls of grass can be compared with a cradle rocker.**"**

# GULLIVER IN LILLIPUT

Retold from Jonathan Swift's *Gulliver's Travels*, this tale illustrates a shipwrecked Englishman's adventures among people six inches tall.

• • • • • • • • • • • • •

66In this version, I wanted the reader to get a sense of the fun Swift must have had in concocting this tale. The spot illustrations bring to mind satirical drawings from Swift's time, but the subtle color relates them to the brighter, full-page pieces in which Gulliver is, in some cases, bursting out a bit. . . . I hope Gulliver looks funny, a bit pompous, but in general, generates sympathy. I enjoyed making up 'egg-related' architecture, which refers to the warring parties in the story.99

*Book Title*
**Gulliver In Lilliput**

*Author*
**Retold by Margaret Hodges**

*Publisher*
**Holiday House**

*Publication Date*
**1995**

*Illustration Medium*
**Pen, ink, and watercolor**

# THE PALACE OF STARS

A young girl treats her great-uncle Max to a Saturday matinee after years of special Saturday outings that were his traditional treat. The story is set in the early 1950s of trolley cars and grand movie theaters.

• • • • • • • • • • • • • • •

66I hoped to show, first, the warmth and depth of the relationship between Amanda and Great-Uncle Max and second—the fabulousness of the old movie palaces. The gestures and facial expressions, and the scenes of interaction between Max and Amanda I hoped would show the first. Reds, purples, golds, Art Deco inspired borders and exaggerated perspectives were what I hoped would show the second.99

*Book Title*
**The Palace of Stars**

*Author*
**Patricia Lakin**

*Publisher*
**Tambourine Books**

*Publication Date*
**1993**

*Illustration Medium*
**Pen, ink, and watercolor**

# ROBERT SABUDA

"My decision to become an illustrator," Robert Sabuda says, "was prompted by my desire not to starve to death". Mr. Sabuda received a Bachelor of Fine Arts in 1987 from Pratt Institute, where he is now an associate professor. His award winning books include *Saint Valentine*, a 1992 Magic Reading Award winner; *Tutankhamen's Gift*, *The New York Times* Outstanding Children's Book, 1994; and *The Christmas Alphabet*, a Blue Ribbon Book from the Center for Children's Books and an American Library Association Notable Book.

## TUTANKHAMEN'S GIFT

A young Egyptian boy becomes pharaoh after the death of his radical older brother, and restores the ancient gods to their former glory.

• • • • • • • • • • • • • •

"I think it's important for the art in a historical picture book to reflect the time period. The challenge with *Tutankhamen's Gift* was creating lively images when in reality, Egyptian art was a bit staid. I thought flowing, cut-paper lines could jazz things up a bit, and the use of papyrus paper underneath just seemed natural. I hope the images evoke a sense of being right in that moment of time, so long ago."

## THE CHRISTMAS ALPHABET

Twenty-six doors, one for each letter of the alphabet, open to reveal a yuletide image in three dimensions.

• • • • • • • • • • • • • •

"You can probably figure out that I'm really 'into paper'. I've never been much of a wet artist. I'm a very tactile person and love the feel of a beautiful or unusual sheet of paper. And pure white paper seemed perfect for Christmas images (although the publisher was a bit nervous). The real challenge, however, with any movable book is the paper engineering. Coming up with twenty-six different visuals and twenty-six engineering mechanisms stretched my creativity to the limit."

*Book Title*
**The Christmas Alphabet**

*Author*
**Robert Sabuda**

*Publisher*
**Orchard Books**

*Publication Date*
**1994**

*Illustration Medium*
**Paper sculpture**

*Book Title*
**Tutankhamen's Gift**

*Author*
**Robert Sabuda**

*Publisher*
**Atheneum Books for Young Readers**

*Publication Date*
**1994**

*Illustration Medium*
**Cut-black paper laid over painted Egyptian papyrus**

## SAINT VALENTINE

An early Christian priest's attempt to cure a girl's blindness leads to his martyrdom and the establishment of Valentine's Day.

● ● ● ● ● ● ● ● ● ● ● ● ● ● ● ●

❝The challenge with this title was that it was a nightmare! Each illustration averaged about 3,500-4,000 pieces of cut paper which had to be individually adhered to the background paper. Yikes! Needless to say, there will not be a sequel.❞

*Book Title*
**Saint Valentine**

*Author*
**Robert Sabuda**

*Publisher*
**Atheneum Books for Young Readers**

*Publication Date*
**1992**

*Illustration Medium*
**Cut-paper mosaic**

# DANIEL SAN SOUCI

Daniel San Souci was born in San Francisco and grew up in Berkeley, California. As a child he had a special interest in literature, and remembers being inspired by the illustrations of Howard Pyle and N.C. Wyeth in the Scribners Classics. His father, who Mr. San Souci says "could draw anything," worked with him in the evenings, helping to develop his artistic talent. After graduating from the California College of Arts and Crafts in Oakland, he collaborated with his brother Robert (who is an award-winning children's book author) on *The Legend of Scarface*—their first book. Since then he has illustrated over forty children's books. Today, Mr. San Souci teaches graduate school and lives with his wife, Loretta, and their three children, Yvette, Justin, and Noël in San Francisco.

*Book Title*
**Jigsaw Jackson**

*Author*
**David F. Birchman**

*Publisher*
**Lothrop, Lee & Shepard Books**

*Publication Date*
**1996**

*Illustration Medium*
**Watercolor**

# JIGSAW JACKSON

J. Jupiter Jackson, a potato farmer, discovers he is a genius at jigsaw puzzles and is convinced by a con man to seek fame and fortune.

• • • • • • • • • • • • • •

❝The characters in my first set of drawings seemed too generic and not humorous enough for the fast-paced, funny text. To solve this problem, I sat down and designed the characters in thumbnail sketches, and used a wooden doll with moving limbs as my new reference for body positions. All of a sudden, my drawings seemed to come to life. The new batch of drawings seemed not only to go along well with David Birchman's clever text, but they also added new twists to the story. . . I executed the paintings in watercolors, using Andrew Wyeth's Maine paintings as inspiration for the backgrounds.❞

# DANIEL SAN SOUCI

*Book Title*
*Sootface: An Ojibwa*
*Cinderella Story*

*Author*
Retold by Robert D. San Souci

*Publisher*
Bantam Books

*Publication Date*
1994

*Illustration Medium*
Watercolor

## SOOTFACE: AN OJIBWA CINDERELLA STORY

Although she is mocked and mistreated by her older sisters, kind and honest Sootface wins the heart of a mighty invisible warrior.

• • • • • • • • • • • • • •

**"**I occasionally paint landscapes on location and they have a certain look and feel to them, and I figured this particular style would work well. My brother Robert, who retold the tale, sent me all the visual information he came across when he was doing his research. This helped me out some, but there were lots of details that seemed almost impossible to find. I spent a great deal of time at the public libraries and also at the University of California library. It was very hard to research a story that took place before the camera was invented, yet when the paintings were completed, I felt like all the hard work really paid off.**"**

# DAVID SHANNON

David Shannon grew up in Spokane, Washington. He graduated from Art Center College of Design in Pasadena, California and moved to New York City, where he began a career in editorial illustration. His work has appeared in *Time, Newsweek, Rolling Stone,* and *The New York Times,* as well as on numerous book jackets. Mr. Shannon illustrated his first children's book, *How Many Spots Does A Leopard Have?* by Julius Lester, thinking it would be an enjoyable diversion from his editorial work. This led to other book projects and the realization that children's books are his passion.

## THE BUNYANS

The story of Paul Bunyan, his wife, and their two children, and how their activities result in the formation of Niagara Falls, Bryce Canyon, and other natural monuments.

• • • • • • • • • • • • • • •

"Since *The Bunyans* dealt with how some of our natural monuments were formed, it gave me a chance to explore landscape painting, which I enjoyed. I felt that Audrey Wood's story was full of just plain ol' good fun, so I wanted to make the characters really, really big. I also tried to keep them interacting with the various settings and with each other. Some of the pages have borders resembling needlepoint or old family album frames to reinforce the idea of the Bunyans as a family."

*Book Title*
**The Amazing Christmas Extravaganza**

*Author*
**David Shannon**

*Publisher*
**The Blue Sky Press**

*Publication Date*
**1995**

*Illustration Medium*
**Acrylic on illustration board**

## THE AMAZING CHRISTMAS EXTRAVAGANZA

Much to the dismay of his neighbors and family, Mr. Merriweather's Christmas display grows from a simple string of white lights into an outrageous spectacle.

• • • • • • • • • • • • • •

&&The biggest challenge of *The Amazing Christmas Extravaganza* was creating all those Christmas lights. It was a lot of fun designing all the decorations, but I've never thought lights were easy to paint. And there were so many of them!&&

*Book Title*
**The Bunyans**

*Author*
**Audrey Wood**

*Publisher*
**The Blue Sky Press**

*Publication Date*
**1996**

*Illustration Medium*
**Acrylic on illustration board**

Anne Bonney          Mary Reade

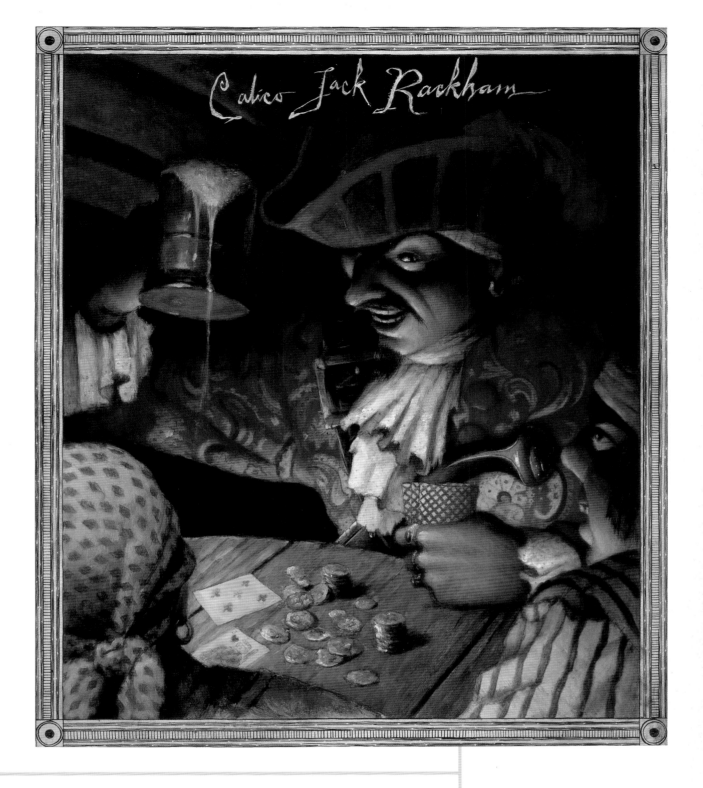

## THE BALLAD OF THE PIRATE QUEENS

The true story of two women pirates who sailed the Caribbean in the early 1700s.

• • • • • • • • • • • • • •

"*The Ballad of the Pirate Queens* was written in the form of a sea chantey, and I wanted the book to reflect this. I decided to make it resemble an old songbook with an engraved title page in pen and ink, hand-lettered captions on the illustrations, and parchment borders and backgrounds. The text was broken up rhythmically, with a two-page spread illustration accompanying each chorus."

Book Title
*The Ballad of the Pirate Queens*

Author
**Jane Yolen**

Publisher
**Harcourt Brace & Company**

Publication Date
**1995**

Illustration Medium
**Acrylic on illustration board**

David Small did not train as an illustrator but as a fine artist. He studied at Wayne State University in Detroit in the late 1960s, and later on at Yale University. Mr. Small taught drawing and printmaking for many years, then university cutbacks forced him into the commercial world where he learned to illustrate for his livelihood. In addition to illustrating children's books, he creates editorial illustrations for magazines and newspapers, lectures at schools, and writes reviews of children's literature for *The New York Times Book Review*. *The Library*, written by David's wife, Sarah Stewart, was *The New York Times* Notable Book of the Year, 1995, and was nominated for the American Booksellers' Book of the Year Award.

## GEORGE WASHINGTON'S COWS

George Washington's cows wear dresses, his pigs serve dinner in livery, and his educated sheep parade around the house in full academic garb. Finally, washing his hands of farming, George tries politics instead.

• • • • • • • • • • • • • •

"I felt the poem (in the tradition of Lewis Carroll and Edward Lear), could be made even more absurd by giving it the authority of the full, classical picture book treatment. In my quest for historical accuracy, I went so far as to travel from Michigan to Virginia and spent many hours at Washington's home at Mount Vernon. There I made endless sketches of architectural details and of the fall of light in rooms. In light of some misgivings I had about treading so irreverently on such hallowed ground, the Mt. Vernon Ladies' Association assured me that George—a man of wit and generosity—would have been the first to laugh at this book."

# FENWICK'S SUIT

A lonely man buys a new suit hoping it will improve his social life. The flamboyant suit comes alive, usurping his life completely.

• • • • • • • • • • • • • • • •

"This fast-paced, screwball comedy required an appropriately loose, streamlined style. To make the three-piece suit come alive, I made it the most vibrant thing in the pictures, knocking back everything else to a monochrome. In addition, the solid, though hidden line of tension between the hero and the suit is a strong anchor for the chaos of details surrounding it. . . . I have done several books with double-page spreads in a horizontal format; within this trim-size, the reader is forced to turn his head to see everything, just as if he or she were sitting in the front row at the movies."

*Book Title*
**Fenwick's Suit**

*Author*
**David Small**

*Publisher*
**Farrar, Straus & Giroux, Inc.**

*Publication Date*
**1996**

*Illustration Medium*
**Colored pencil**

*Book Title*
**George Washington's Cows**

*Author*
**David Small**

*Publisher*
**Farrar, Straus & Giroux, Inc.**

*Publication Date*
**1994**

*Illustration Medium*
**Pen, ink, and watercolor on Arches hot-pressed paper**

*Book Title*
**The Library**

*Author*
**Sarah Stewart**

*Publisher*
**Farrar, Straus & Giroux, Inc.**

*Publication Date*
**1995**

*Illustration Medium*
**Watercolor**

## THE LIBRARY

Young and strongly independent Elizabeth Brown's greatest love is reading. As she grows up, her collection of books becomes so tremendous, that she eventually makes a grand donation to the public library.

• • • • • • • • • • • • • •

66 This book posed a serious illustration problem because watching someone read is about as exciting as watching a painting dry. My first idea was to make the art splashy and energetic, with pictures bleeding off the edges of each page and with text worked into the art. It was dreadful. I threw everything away and started over again. The author (my wife), had always asked for the book to have the look and feel of an old-fashioned library; that is, safe, enclosed, quiet. When I hit upon the idea of multiple hairline borders framing both the pictures and the text, I realized that we had arrived at the same conclusion by different routes. The borders give that feeling of safety and enclosure, as well as a dignity which my former art (now in the trash), entirely lacked. I went back to review the suggestions in John Ruskin's book *The Elements of Drawing*, on how to paint with watercolor. 99

# BRAD SNEED

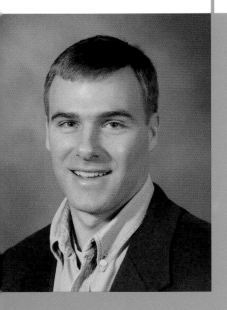

Brad Sneed has been working as a freelance illustrator since he graduated in 1989 from Kansas University with a Bachelor of Fine Arts degree. His work has been exhibited at the Society of Illustrators in New York and The Chemers Gallery in California. In addition to his work on picture books, Mr. Sneed's illustrations have appeared in ads for Hilton Hotels, Mercantile Bank and the Indiana Lottery, as well as in *Country Life*, *American Bookseller*, and *Inside Sports* magazines. He lives with his wife and daughter in Prairie Village, Kansas and is busy working on his next book.

*Book Title*
**Lucky Russell**

*Author*
**Brad Sneed**

*Publisher*
**G.P. Putnam's Sons**

*Publication Date*
**1992**

*Illustration Medium*
**Watercolor**

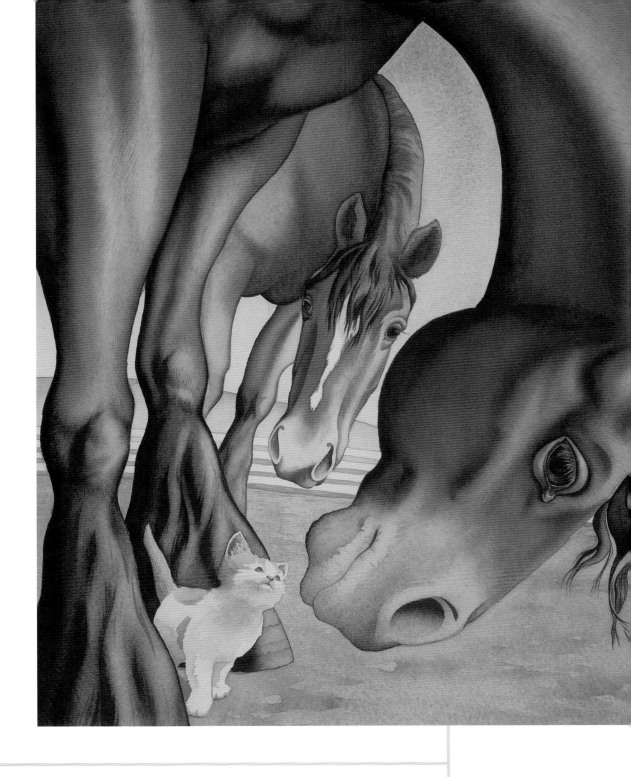

## LUCKY RUSSELL

Russell the kitten is sad because while he is stuck having "tea" with the farmer's daughter, the other animals seem to have big, important jobs to do. He sets out to find a job that is just right for him.

• • • • • • • • • • • • •

❝It was a special joy to create pictures for this book, as *Lucky Russell* is a story that I wrote. In the story, the kitten visits each farm animal individually and asks if he can help them with their particular job. It was a challenge to show Russell next to one animal after another and avoid redundancy. I chose to vary the viewpoints of each scene, altering the composition so that each painting is unique, yet maintains a cohesiveness with the artwork throughout the book. By bending the perspectives and exaggerating shapes and sizes of the animals and barnyard, I hope to help the reader identify with Russell's feeling of insignificance.❞

# GENNADY SPIRIN

Gennady Spirin was born in Moscow in 1948 and now lives in the United States. When he was a boy, his favorite book was *Gulliver's Travels*, and illustrating this beloved classic was the fulfillment of a lifelong dream. His meticulously researched illustrations have brought him international renown and many distinguished awards, including *The New York Times* Best Illustrated Book Award, 1993 for *Gulliver's Adventures in Lilliput*.

*Book Title*
**Gulliver's Adventures in Lilliput**

*Author*
**Retold by Ann Keay Beneduce**

*Publisher*
**Philomel Books**

*Publication Date*
**1993**

*Illustration Medium*
**Watercolor and pencil**

## GULLIVER'S ADVENTURES IN LILLIPUT

This story is retold from Jonathan Swift's classic novel, set in 1699. Dr. Lemuel Gulliver, shipwrecked, is captured by a race of tiny people no taller than his finger.

• • • • • • • • • • • • • •

**"**Obviously, the contrast in dimensions between the tiny, but perfectly formed Lilliputians and the much larger Gulliver was the primary challenge in illustrating this classic story. Careful research was needed to re-create the costumes, ships, and architecture of the period, and to lend it a feeling of authenticity. I designed the pages to underline a nautical theme, placing the text on halyards, and decorating borders with knots and anchors. I executed the art in many layers of transparent watercolors over careful drawings in pencil. I tried to bring out Gulliver's adventurous character, and to show his emotional responses to the remarkable situations in which he found himself, hoping the child reader would identify with the hero in his courage and zest for adventure.**"**

# JANET STEVENS

Janet Stevens studied fine arts at the University of Colorado. In 1977, after attending an illustrator's workshop in New York City, she was introduced to the field of children's books. Tomie dePaola was instrumental in launching Ms. Stevens' career, encouraging her to stick with book illustration and introducing her to the publishing houses. Her books have won state awards in Nevada, Washington State, Indiana, and Colorado; and she is the recipient of the Caldecott Honor Award, 1996 for *Tops and Bottoms*. Ms. Stevens' original art has appeared in the Society of Illustrators show in New York City and hangs in the Mazza collection at the University of Findlay.

*Book Title*
***Anansi and the Talking Melon***

*Author*
**Eric Kimmel**

*Publisher*
**Holiday House**

*Publication Date*
**1994**

*Illustration Medium*
**Watercolor and colored pencil**

# ANANSI AND THE TALKING MELON

Anansi the spider eats so much of the inside of a melon that he can't get out. When he talks to the animals, they bring this "talking melon" to the king.

• • • • • • • • • • • • • • •

❝Drawing Anansi inside the melon and speaking to the other characters were major challenges. I decided to show a cross section of the melon at times and at other times, to show Anansi's head poking out of the hole in the melon. Children seem most concerned that I chose a gorilla for the king in this book. Naturally they think a lion should be king. But Lion appears in *Anansi and the Moss-Covered Rock* and he is not king. I thought it would make more sense for a new character to wear the crown.❞

# JANET STEVENS

Book Title
**Coyote Steals the Blanket**

Author
**Retold by Janet Stevens**

Publisher
**Holiday House**

Publication Date
**1993**

Illustration Medium
**Watercolor, oil pastel, and colored pencil**

Book Title
**Tops and Bottoms**

Author
**Retold by Janet Stevens**

Publisher
**Harcourt Brace & Company**

Publication Date
**1995**

Illustration Medium
**Watercolor, gesso, and colored pencil on hand-made paper**

## TOPS AND BOTTOMS

A poor hare strikes a clever deal with a rich, lazy bear. With its roots in the slave stories of the American South, this story celebrates the trickster tradition of overcoming hardship with one's wits.

• • • • • • • • • • • • • •

66 The vertical format of *Tops and Bottoms* shifted my composition from the start. The book is a trickster tale about the planting and harvesting of vegetables, so I decided to paint the art on hand-made clothes—a challenging and exciting texture to work on. The bear character was particularly interesting to render. He sleeps for most of the book in his porch chair and only shifts positions. 99

## COYOTE STEALS THE BLANKET

A trickster tale from the Ute Tribe. Coyote takes a blanket from a rock, wears it for a new coat, and is chased by the rock from which he stole it.

• • • • • • • • • • • • • • • • •

66 *Coyote Steals the Blanket* is a book about a chase. I tried to evoke speed with the pacing of smaller and larger illustrations. At times, Coyote darts off the edge of the page. The desert setting and color was an exciting backdrop, and I used a loose drawing style to enhance the movement and manginess of Coyote. It is my hope the reader will feel the energy and humor of the coyote character. 99

# MARK C. TEAGUE

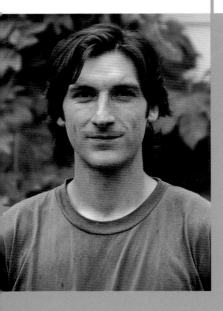

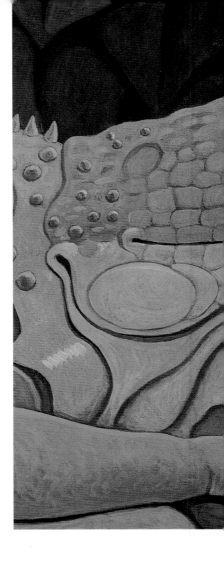

*Book Title*
**The Iguana Brothers**

*Author*
**Tony Johnston**

*Publisher*
**The Blue Sky Press**

*Publication Date*
**1995**

*Illustration Medium*
**Acrylic on hot press watercolor paper**

*Book Title*
**Pigsty**

*Author*
**Mark C. Teague**

*Publisher*
**Scholastic Inc.**

*Publication Date*
**1993**

*Illustration Medium*
**Acrylic on cold press watercolor paper**

After Mark C. Teague graduated from the University of California, Santa Cruz with a history degree, he moved to New York City "without any clear ambitions." There he found a job doing display work for Barnes & Noble, giving him some art training and exposure to children's books. In 1988, Mr. Teague's first book, *The Trouble with the Johnsons*, was published. He is the recipient of the Parents' Choice Illustration Honor Award for *Pigsty*, 1994 and the Oppenheim Toy Portfolio Platinum Award, 1995. Much of Mr. Teague's work is currently on consignment to the Storyopolis gallery in Los Angeles.

## PIGSTY

A fantasy springing from a mother's complaint about the condition of her son's bedroom. The room literally becomes a pigsty when a group of pigs takes up residence.

• • • • • • • • • • • • • •

❝The illustrations needed to be energetic to provide a counterpoint to the deadpan text and to counteract the story's main visual limitation—it takes place almost entirely inside a single messy room. Although the color scheme is somewhat limited, I chose colors that would enhance the exaggerated pinkness of the pigs. And just in case it began to feel claustrophobic, I let the characters jump out of the frame from time to time.❞

## THE IGUANA BROTHERS

*The Iguana Brothers* live in Mexico, eat bugs, entertain delusions of grandeur (they convince themselves they're dinosaurs) and ultimately learn about friendship.

• • • • • • • • • • • • • •

❝Most of the humor of this story is contained in the dialogue between the two lizards. There isn't a great deal of action, so I tried to convey movement by shifting perspective, and create energy with splashes of bright tropical color.❞

Classmates in college, Jean and Mou-sien Tseng both received their Bachelor of Fine Arts from the National Taiwan Normal University. They have both been teachers and artists, as well as illustrators. Mou-sien won the Golden Book Award in the Best Children's Book Illustration category, and also received the Golden Goblet Award for outstanding achievement in Chinese painting from the Art Society of China. *The Seven Chinese Brothers* received *Parenting* magazine's Reading Magic Award for distinguished achievement in children's literature, and is an American Library Association Notable Book.

## THE SEVEN CHINESE BROTHERS

Seven identical brothers, with their individual extraordinary powers, elude execution and conquer a tyrant.

. . . . . . . . . . . . . . .

66We think that illustrating a book together is a wonderful, exciting, and challenging process. Through the sharing and development of different ideas, we come to a consensus on a final product which combines the best of each unique perspective. While we celebrate our individuality and the difference that it brings, we also marvel at how two minds can have so much in common and be so different at the same time.99

*Book Title*
**The Khan's Daughter: A Mongolian Folktale**

*Author*
**Laurence Yep**

*Publisher*
**Scholastic Inc.**

*Publication Date*
**1997**

*Illustration Medium*
**Watercolor on Arches paper**

## THE KHAN'S DAUGHTER: A MONGOLIAN FOLKTALE

This story takes place in Mongolia—a place with fascinating images of vast grassland, horses, horsemen, warriors, and Genghis Khan.

• • • • • • • • • • • • • •

66 We travelled to inner Mongolia, and it left us with beautiful and vivid memories. To illustrate this story was like a dream come true, and we were thrilled to have the chance to share our wonderful experience with all readers who are young at heart. 99

*Book Title*
**The Seven Chinese Brothers**

*Author*
**Margaret Mahy**

*Publisher*
**Scholastic Inc.**

*Publication Date*
**1990**

*Illustration Medium*
**Watercolor on Arches paper**

# JEAN & MOU-SIEN TSENG

*Book Title*
**The River Dragon**

*Author*
**Darcy Pattison**

*Publisher*
**Lothrop, Lee & Shepard Books**

*Publication Date*
**1991**

*Illustration Medium*
**Watercolor on Arches paper**

## THE RIVER DRAGON

Ying Shao must make three dangerous trips across the river dragon's bridge before he can marry the lovely Kal-Li.

● ● ● ● ● ● ● ● ● ● ● ● ● ●

66After exchanging preliminary ideas about the manuscript, and thorough research, we started by working on separate thumbnail sketches. When these rough sketches were completed, we reviewed our work by telling the story to each other through the drawings. After much repetition, negotiation, and some luck, the most suitable drawings for each page were determined. Then we went on to sketches in original size, while slowly adding detail and color.99

# NEIL WALDMAN

## THE TYGER

A picture book rendition of William Blake's famous poem.

• • • • • • • • • • • • •

"I feel that if I am able to immerse myself fully in any story, and listen to the words like a child hearing its first story, then each book I do will be unique. The story always tells me which medium to use. . . . One afternoon, while lying on the couch with a terrible headache, the image for *The Tyger* suddenly flooded my inner eye. The book would be comprised of one huge mural depicting many images described in the poem. The reader would see one small segment of the mural on each page. But the entire tiger wouldn't be revealed until the end of the book. I also knew I would paint it with acrylics on canvas, and that the style would be primitive, similar to a Henry Rousseau."

Neil Waldman has been an illustrator for 25 years, and began creating picture books in the 1980s. "I love illustrating," Mr. Waldman says, "because I get the same joy I felt as a child using finger paints in kindergarten". In 1986, he entered a competition in which artists from eight countries created posters for the United Nations' "International Year of Peace". Mr. Waldman's painting was awarded the gold medal— the prize of which he is most proud.

*Book Title*
**The Tyger**

*Author*
**William Blake**

*Publisher*
**Harcourt Brace & Company**

*Publication Date*
**1993**

*Illustration Medium*
**Acrylic on canvas**

NEIL WALDMAN

Book Title
**The Never-Ending
Greenness**

Author
**Neil Waldman**

Publisher
**Morrow Junior Books**

Publication Date
**1997**

Illustration Medium
**Acrylic on watercolor paper**

# THE NEVER-ENDING GREENNESS

The story of a young boy who journeys through World War II Europe to Israel, where he becomes a tree planter. It is also the story of the power of dreams to create our reality.

· · · · · · · · · · · · · ·

**❝**I used to live in Israel, and whenever I rode past the forests in the Judean Hills, my pulse would quicken. I knew that the trees had been planted by people, and that not long ago, all the hills were barren. I especially remember a walk I took one April morning in the mountains outside Jerusalem. I was passing through a grove of pine trees, when I came upon hundreds of tiny seedlings, springing up on the forest floor. It was absolutely thrilling, because these newly planted forests were regenerating naturally. It seemed like a miracle to me. I spent the rest of that day running through the hills, in a euphoric state that only nature can inspire. The thrill of that day has remained with me, and it provided the inspiration for this book.**❞**

# JEANETTE WINTER

Jeanette Winter was born in Chicago, Illinois in 1939 and studied at the Art Institute of Chicago and the University of Iowa. In 1960, she married Roger Winter, a painter, with whom she had two children—Jonah and Max. Ms. Winter is the recipient of the Parents' Choice Award, Notable Children's Trade Book in the field of social studies, and *The New York Times* Best Illustrated Children's Book Award, 1991 for *Diego*, which was also a Reading Rainbow feature selection. For *Klara's New World*, she received the International Reading Association Award, Teachers' Choice Award and Parents' Choice Award, 1992.

*Book Title*
**Cowboy Charlie**

*Author*
**Jeanette Winter**

*Publisher*
**Harcourt Brace & Company**

*Publication Date*
**1995**

*Illustration Medium*
**Acrylics**

## COWBOY CHARLIE

The story of Charles M. Russell, the cowboy artist, who left St. Louis as a boy to become a cowboy in Montana. He went on to become a famous artist of the wild West.

• • • • • • • • • • • • • •

66 The biggest challenge was to give a sense of the western landscape, and still keep the book to a moderate trim size. I wanted the pictures to reflect how Charlie Russell saw the West as his own kind of paradise, and as inspiration for his paintings. . . . I like to work in acrylic. It is a medium that is forgiving, and changes can be made easily. This allows me to concentrate on telling the story, mainly with image and color. 99

# KLARA'S NEW WORLD

The story of a young Swedish girl and her parents who emigrate to America in the 19th century and settle in Minnesota.

• • • • • • • • • • • • • • •

❝The main challenge of *Klara's New World* was to tell of an epic journey with a limited number of pictures. I hoped the pictures would convey the enormity of such a journey for a family—the sense of loss at leaving home, the hardships of travel, and being strangers in a new land.❞

*Book Title*
**Klara's New World**

*Author*
**Jeanette Winter**

*Publisher*
**Alfred A. Knopf, Inc.**

*Publication Date*
**1992**

*Illustration Medium*
**Acrylics**

*Book Title*
**Diego**

*Author*
**Jeanette Winter**

*Publisher*
**Alfred A. Knopf, Inc.**

*Publication Date*
**1991**

*Illustration Medium*
**Acrylics**

# DIEGO

*Diego* is a biography of Diego Rivera, the Mexican muralist, for young children.

• • • • • • • • • • • • • •

❝One of the main challenges was to simplify rather complicated concepts, such as the Mexican Revolution and art study in Europe, for young children. I hoped that the book would give children a sense of Mexico, and also the single-mindedness, curiosity, and grand ambition of an artist like Rivera. The small scale of my pictures contrasts with the scale of the murals Rivera painted. Also, the small scale intensifies the color.❞

David Wisniewski graduated from the Ringling Brothers and Barnum & Bailey Clown College in 1972. After years of touring with tent shows, he was hired as a puppeteer in 1976. Six months later, he married. In 1980, he and his wife founded their own shadow theater troupe—the Clarion Shadow Theater—and toured throughout the United States. This style of puppetry, which required cutting techniques and a familiarity with myths and legends, helped develop all the skills Mr. Wisniewski would later use in his children's books. All his books have been invited to the Original Art Exhibition at the Society of Illustrators. Mr. Wisniewski is the recipient of the Biennale of Illustrations Bratislava Award, 1991 and the *New York Times* Best Illustrated Children's Book, 1996, and the Caldecott Award, 1997 for *Golem*.

*Book Title*
**Golem**

*Author*
**David Wisniewski**

*Publisher*
**Clarion Books**

*Publication Date*
**1996**

*Illustration Medium*
**Cut-paper illustration**

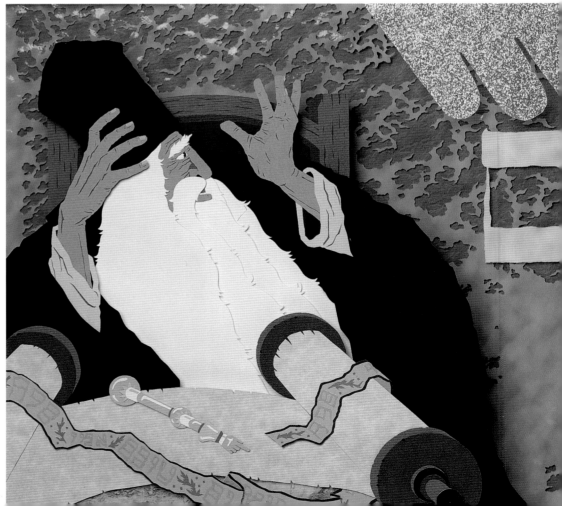

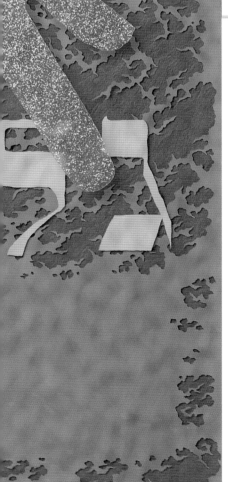

## GOLEM

The chief rabbi of Prague uses magic to create a golem—a giant of living clay to protect his people from harm.

· · · · · · · · · · · · · · · ·

❝The Hand of God is a stage effect called 'sparklene'—an iridescent self-adhesive plastic. It's stuck to a piece of shower door plexiglass placed over the gray background and Hebrew lettering, giving a dreamy, mottled effect. . . . I've always liked big bombastic stories with lots of peril and consequence. This probably comes from having learned how to draw from *Marvel Comics*. Be that as it may, it's very important to have cultural accuracy and a moral point of view. Then the payoff really matters. It's not just satisfactory; it has resonance.❞

# DAVID WISNIEWSKI

*Book Title*
**Elfwyn's Saga**

*Author*
**David Wisniewski**

*Publisher*
**Lothrop, Lee & Shepard Books**

*Publication Date*
**1990**

*Illustration Medium*
**Cut-paper illustration**

## ELFWYN'S SAGA

Blinded by an evil curse, a Viking girl's uncanny abilities (granted by the fairy-folk of Icelandic legend) enable her to defeat a ferocious warrior and regain her sight.

• • • • • • • • • • • • • •

"Faced with a heroine undergoing daunting challenges, the silhouette style had to give way to more fully realized figures. Lee Salsbery, the photographer of all the books, suggested layering the paper with greater depth so that he could achieve more pronounced shadow effects. Accomplishing these technical feats made this book the most arduous to produce, but solidified my style."

# THE WARRIOR AND THE WISE MAN

Twin brothers pursue opposing methods of force and thought to earn the right to govern medieval Japan.

66 For this archetypal tale of twin brothers pursuing opposing methods of force and wisdom to win their father's throne, the silhouettes I'd become adept at cutting through years of shadow puppetry served the story well. This opening spread depicts the dual nature of the twin while establishing place and mood. 99

*Book Title*
**The Warrior and the Wise Man**

*Author*
**David Wisniewski**

*Publisher*
**Lothrop, Lee & Shepard Books**

*Publication Date*
**1989**

*Illustration Medium*
**Cut-paper illustration**

# DAN YACCARINO

Since his graduation from Parsons School of Design in 1987, Dan Yaccarino has been creating images for magazines, newspapers, and ad campaigns in the United States and around the world. His free-wheeling and lighthearted illustrations were natural for children's books, and in 1992 he wrote and illustrated his first book, *Big Brother Mike*.

*Book Title*
*One Hole in the Road*

*Author*
**W. Nikola-Lisa**

*Publisher*
**Henry Holt and Company, Inc.**

*Publication Date*
**1996**

*Illustration Medium*
**Gouache on watercolor paper**

## ONE HOLE IN THE ROAD

Trying to fix a small pothole is apparently no easy task. Flagmen, barricades, flashing lights, sirens and engineers only seem to make the problem worse.

• • • • • • • • • • • • •

"This book was a turning point in the way I approach my work. It took great pains for me to pare the illustrations down to their most essential elements: shape and color. What appears to be the simplest of images is the result of much deliberation and discarded illustrations."

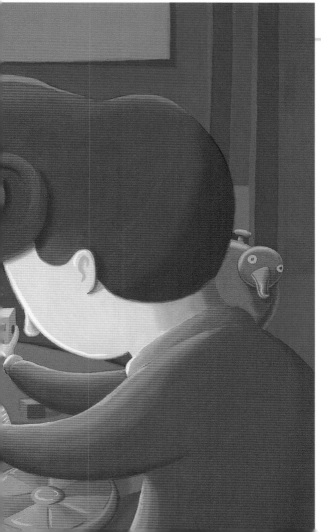

# BIG BROTHER MIKE

A young boy relays the trials and tribulations of having an older brother who, in the end, likes him after all.

● ● ● ● ● ● ● ● ● ● ● ● ● ●

**"**The question I am most asked in regard to this book is, 'do you have an older brother?' Isn't it obvious? And, by the way, yes, his name is Mike. I wanted to show what it's like to be the younger sibling and all the problems there are being 'the baby'. I also hoped to show all the good things that go along with it, too.**"**

*Book Title*
**Big Brother Mike**

*Author*
**Dan Yaccarino**

*Publisher*
**Hyperion Books for Children**

*Publication Date*
**1993**

*Illustration Medium*
**Gouache on watercolor paper**

# DIRK ZIMMER

*Book Title*
**One Eye, Two Eyes, Three Eyes: A Hutzul Tale**

*Author*
**Retold by Eric A. Kimmel**

*Publisher*
**Holiday House**

*Publication Date*
**1996**

*Illustration Medium*
**Watercolor and linocut**

Dirk Zimmer grew up in Hamburg, West Germany, where he started in early childhood to draw and tell picture stories. During the 1960s he visited the Academy of Fine Art in Hamburg and sneered at all commercial art. When he got stuck in New York City one day in 1977 and had to earn some money to buy a ticket back to Germany, he made an exception and created some drawings for *The New York Times*. There, his illustration was noticed ("a silly thing depicting dancing sausages") and he was offered a job illustrating *Felix in the Attic*, which promptly won the Bank Street College of Education Award.

## ONE EYE, TWO EYES, THREE EYES: A HUTZUL TALE

To honor her father's promise, a young girl agrees to become the slave of a witch and her two daughters, enduring their cruelty with the help of her talking pet goat.

• • • • • • • • • • • • • •

66Besides using hard-to-decipher visual material for a Hutzul atmosphere, I tried to evoke the imagery of an 'archetypal' forest, partly with linocuts printed into the watercolor work to achieve a blend of individuality and anonymity.99

# DIRK ZIMMER

## THE IRON GIANT

A fearsome iron giant, who terrorizes farmers and townspeople with his insatiable hunger for metal, suddenly becomes a hero when he challenges a huge space monster.

· · · · · · · · · · · · · · · ·

"This story was commisioned by the publisher to be done in black-and-white drawings—the medium in which I began illustrating children's books. I originally intended to try etchings and metal prints for the book. Using black ink instead was more practical, and still enabled me to formulate an easily repeatable design for the giant."

*Book Title*
**Bony Legs**

*Author*
**Joanna Cole**

*Publisher*
**Simon & Schuster Books
for Young Readers**

*Publication Date*
**1983**

*Illustration Medium*
**Black-and-white drawings
and color separations**

## BONY LEGS

When a terrible witch vows to eat a little girl for supper, she escapes with help from the witch's cat and dog.

• • • • • • • • • • • • • •

**66**This story is based on a Russian fairy tale called 'Baba-Yaga'. I researched a great deal, and used a lot of imagery from books by Ivan Bilibin in *Bony Legs*, which has some of his flair. This story incorporates folklore and tradition, more so than in any of my other books. Although it changed publishers three times, it went on to become my bestselling book. **99**

*Book Title*
**The Iron Giant**

*Author*
**Ted Hughes**

*Publisher*
**HarperCollins Publishers**

*Publication Date*
**1988**

*Illustration Medium*
**Black ink**

# CREDITS

# PUBLISHERS

**Bantam Doubleday Dell Publishing Group, Inc.**
*Bantam Books*
1540 Broadway
New York, New York 10036
United States
Tel: (212) 782-8815
Fax: (212) 782-8898

**Disney Book Publishing, Inc.**
*Hyperion Books for Children*
114 Fifth Avenue
New York, New York 10011
United States
Tel: (212) 633-4400
Fax: (212) 727-4879

**Farrar, Straus & Giroux, Inc.**
19 Union Square West
New York, New York 10003
United States
Tel: (212) 741-6900
Fax: (212) 741-6973

**Harcourt Brace & Company**
6277 Sea Harbor Drive
Orlando, Florida 32887-6777
United States
Tel: (407) 345-2000
Fax: (407) 352-3445

**HarperCollins Publishers**
10 East 53rd Street
New York, New York 10022-5299
United States
Tel: (212) 207-7217
Fax: (212) 207-7939

**Holiday House**
425 Madison Avenue
New York, New York 10017
United States
Tel: (212) 688-0085
Fax: (212) 421-6134

**Henry Holt and Company, Inc.**
115 West 18th Street
New York, New York 10011
United States
Tel: (212) 886-9200
Fax: (212) 633-0748

**Houghton Mifflin Company**
*Clarion Books*
215 Park Avenue South
New York, New York 10003
United States
Tel: (212) 420-5800
Fax: (212) 420-5899

**Alfred A. Knopf, Inc.**
201 East 50th Street
New York, New York 10022
United States
Tel: (212) 751-2600
Fax: (212) 572-2593

**Little, Brown and Company**
34 Beacon Street
Boston, Massachusetts 02108-1493
United States
Tel: (617) 227-0730
Fax: (617) 227-4633

**William Morrow & Company, Inc.**
*Lothrop, Lee & Shepard Books*
*Morrow Junior Books*
*Tambourine Books*
1350 Avenue of the Americas
New York, New York 10019
United States
Tel: (212) 261-6500
Fax: (212) 261-6595

**North-South Books Inc.**
1123 Broadway
New York, New York 10010
United States
Tel: (212) 463-9736
Fax: (212) 633-1004

**Orchard Books**
95 Madison Avenue
New York, New York 10016
United States
Tel: (212) 951-2600
Fax: (212) 213-6435

**The Putnam & Grosset Group**
*G.P. Putnam's Sons*
*Philomel Books*
200 Madison Avenue
New York, New York 10016
United States
Tel: (212) 951-8700
Fax: (212) 532-3693

**Random House, Inc.**
*Crown Publishers, Inc.*
201 East 50th Street
New York, New York 10022
United States
Tel: (212) 751-2600
Fax: (212) 572-8700

**Scholastic Inc.**
*The Blue Sky Press*
555 Broadway
New York, New York 10012-3999
United States
Tel: (212) 343-6100
Fax: (212) 343-6930

**Simon & Schuster**
*Atheneum Books for Young Readers*
*Margaret K. McElderry Books*
*Simon & Schuster Books for Young Readers*
1633 Broadway
New York, New York 10019
United States
Tel: (212) 654-7502
Fax: (212) 654-4782

# INDEX